# CELTIC

## THE JOCK STEIN YEARS

# CELTIC

## THE JOCK STEIN YEARS

### Graham McColl

Foreword by
DANNY McGRAIN

First published in Great Britain in 1999 by Chameleon Books
an imprint of André Deutsch Limited
76 Dean Street
London W1V 5HA
HYPERLINK http://www.vci.co.uk

Published under licence from Celtic Football Club

Published in association with
The Memorabilia Pack Company
16 Forth Street
Edinburgh EH1 3LH

10 9 8 7 6 5 4 3 2 1

Printed in Hong Kong by Dah Hua Printing Press Co. Ltd

A catalogue record for this book is available from the British Library

ISBN 0 233 99615 X

Cover design by Words and Pictures
Page design by Design 23

**DEDICATION**
For Jackie

**ACKNOWLEDGEMENTS**
I would like to thank Nicky Paris and Kerrin Edwards at André Deutsch for their special help in putting this book together. I would also like to thank Danny McGrain for his foreword and Jim Craig, Billy McNeill, John Divers, John Hughes, Tommy Gemmell and Jimmy Johnstone for their time and help in interviews. Thanks also to Hal Norman, copy editor.
The newspaper archive at the Mitchell Library provided an endless fund of information. For this book, back issues of the *Glasgow Herald*, the *Scotsman*, the *Daily Record* and the *Sunday Telegraph* proved extremely useful.
The Memorabilia Pack Company would like to thank the following people for their assistance: Derek Taylor (Kollectables, Glasgow), John Johnstone, Celtic Football Club, the *Daily Record*, the *Sunday Mail*, Margaret McCuiag, Stuart Marshall, Jack Murray, and the Scottish Football Association.

**PICTURE CREDITS**
COVER PHOTOGRAPHS
memorabilia photograph by Chris Hall
© D.C. Thomson & Co. Ltd; © MSI; The Sun/ Science and Society Picture Library; © Colorsport.

© D.C. Thomson & Co. Ltd; 1, 2, 6, 15, 18, 20, 23, 27, 28, 31, 34, 35, 50, 51, 52, 62, 64, 84, 87, 89, 90, 92; Eric McCowat Photography: 59, 61a, 70a, 70b, 76, 82, 85, 90, 96; © MSI: 10-11, 24, 32, 33, 36, 38, 44, 49, 54, 69, 73, 77, 80, 95; Popperfoto: 9, 16, 55, 61b, 65, 88; *Daily Herald* Archive NMPFT/Science and Society Picture Library: 13, 47, 60; *The Sun*/Science and Society Picture Library: 19, 57; *Manchester Daily Express*/Science and Society Picture Library: 30, 66, 74; Associated Press/Science and Society Picture Library: 41.

# CONTENTS

# FOREWORD by Danny McGrain

MY FIRST POWERFUL MEMORY OF MR STEIN IS OF WATCHING THE 1967 EUROPEAN CUP FINAL ON television. Three months later I had my first meeting with Mr Stein. I was offered a part-time contract and went to Celtic Park to sign the forms. When I met Mr Stein he was such a big man that he seemed like a giant. He had such an aura about him. I didn't see him

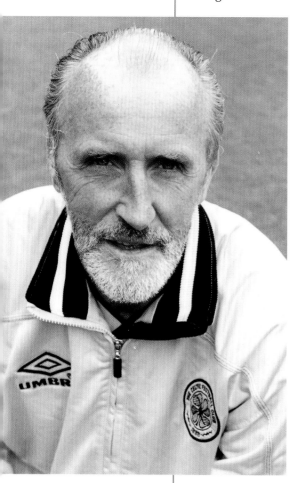

Danny McGrain

again until the following year, because I was only training two nights a week. Then Kenny Dalglish and I had a discussion between ourselves; Kenny had also joined as a part-timer in 1967. We agreed that we would ask Mr Stein if we could go full-time.

When I met him in his office, Mr Stein did not put any pressure on me. He simply asked me if I was sure I wanted to go full-time, as that would mean giving up my college studies. I told him I wanted to put all my energy and imagination into playing football. After he emphasised another couple of times that I had to be sure about my decision he told me the club would take me on as a full-time player. I left his office without asking about wages or a signing-on fee or any other business. I think I felt so much respect for Mr Stein, mixed with some fear, that I did not feel confident enough to approach him about such matters.

Although new players like myself had respect for Mr Stein from a distance, we could also see that the Lisbon Lions, with whom he worked on a daily basis, also had great respect for him. He would be continually talking to people and getting the best out of them. There was also a big, soft part to him. When he talked to you it was like your granda talking to you. You were never really scared of him as a person, you just feared that you would not have done the right thing for him. I think we were always looking for praise and acceptance from Mr Stein.

At the age of 17 or 18 you didn't really appreciate how exceptional Mr Stein's style of management was; you realized that only when you learned about other managers. Some managers just shout and bawl at people, then come a Saturday they want you to play for them. Mr Stein used persuasion although, if he was pushed, he could bawl you out as loudly as anyone.

When it came to tactics and how to play the game, Mr Stein simplified things beautifully. When I was a youngster, I was sometimes only aware of the right-hand side of the park. He made me fully aware of the opportunity to use the left-hand side of the park. That might sound simple but before that it had been as if I had been wearing an eye-patch over my left eye. At right-back I would play the ball either long or short up the right. One day at training he took me aside and told me to look for options on the left-hand side of the field. I told him that during a game I did not have time to look left but he said, 'You do have time if you look over before the ball comes to you.'

So Mr Stein would play the ball to me and tell me to aim a pass at Bertie Auld on the left. The first couple of times I was off-target but he kept encouraging me. Then I found I could hit a crossfield pass and now had a whole lot of options I hadn't had before. It seemed so simple and I said to myself, 'Why didn't I think of that before?' It was another example of Mr Stein teaching me to look at the whole picture instead of just the right-hand side of the picture or the centre of the picture. I learned that lesson within ten minutes and it stuck with me throughout my career.

In the next match I tried a crossfield pass three times; once it was cut out and twice it reached its target. I was delighted but after the game Mr Stein said nothing. On the Monday at our Barrowfield training ground he just said, 'It worked, didn't it?' That was all the praise I needed because he was never one for going overboard or backslapping. And his methods worked. As soon as Mr Stein asked you to do something you would find you could do it because you had such belief in his judgement. You knew that he would not ask you to do anything of which you were incapable.

He taught me about respect for other people, which I think he had. I never once heard him say anything disrespectful about our opponents, regardless of the importance of the match. He was also very self-disciplined – I never saw Mr Stein take a drink – and he expected good discipline from other people. In disciplinary matters he would give the individual concerned a little tip to get their life under control – he wouldn't shout at them or lay down the law. He would always give people the opportunity to step back from the brink. It was then up to the player concerned to take the tip but if they failed to do so they would soon find there was no room for them in Mr Stein's team.

He was great fun at training. He thoroughly enjoyed racing around, laying balls off for people to shoot at goal and giving out stick. He was a great, distinctive figure, with his bulk. Sometimes Sean Fallon or Neilly Mochan would be taking training in Mr Stein's absence. Then when Mr Stein appeared you would suddenly find everyone running a lot more quickly and tidying up their appearance.

He loved the game. He loved going to watch First Division games, Second Division games, whatever. Mr Stein would love to sit in the stand at one of these games and I'm sure he took things from these wee games that he applied to the bigger stage.

After he became manager of Scotland, in 1978, I got to know him even better as a person. Then, in 1980, he was on my testimonial committee. That led to the only time I ever addressed him as 'Jock'. I always call him Mr Stein because I can't call him anything else. At the presentation of gifts from my committee I stood up and said, 'It's the first time I've ever called this guy by his first name…' Then I said, 'Right, Jock, up you come…' It was just a small presentation but on that one occasion I felt so awkward calling him 'Jock'. It didn't feel right so that was the only time I ever called him by his first name. Even now I can't call him 'Jock' or 'The big man'. I just can't.

I was in awe of Mr Stein until the day he died. I only wish that he was here today to talk to modern managers and for them to learn from him. I miss Mr Stein because I have nobody really of his ilk from whom I can ask advice. There will never be anyone like him again. I'm quite sure of that.

# INTRODUCTION

Jock Stein is as much a part of Celtic's present as its past. That was emphasised on 8 August 1998, when Celtic's new west stand was opened and named after the man who had been the club's greatest manager. It was the first time in Celtic's by then 110-year history that any terracing or stand in the ground had been named in honour of one individual. Twenty years after Jock Stein's final departure from the club, his widow, Jean, cut the ribbon to formally open the new edifice.

That warm afternoon, the Celtic fans spontaneously broke into 'Jock Stein, Jock Stein', a gentle, respectful chant of affection for a man who gave so much of his life to the club. Their appreciative gesture showed how the significance of Stein's time as manager remains firmly etched in the hearts and minds of all those with a Celtic connection. The west stand was the final part in the construction of the new all-seated Celtic Park, which is entirely unrecognisable from the basic stand and terraces that Stein looked out on when he took control at the club in 1965. Yet while the supporters' surroundings may have changed, the emotional links between their club's past and present are continually reinforced, most particularly by their awareness of Jock Stein's magnificent achievements.

Exactly twenty years previously, in August 1978, Stein had taken to the Celtic pitch for the final time to acknowledge the Celtic support at his testimonial match, also against Liverpool. Accompanying him were his Lisbon Lions, the Celtic men who had won the European Cup a decade previously. In the Liverpool team was Kenny Dalglish, who had scored the winning goal in the European Cup final in May 1978. Stein's careful tuition had helped provide Dalglish with the qualities that would lead him to become Britain's most complete footballer. As the forward himself said, the best education any young player could have had was to work with Jock Stein on a daily basis.

The achievements of Celtic under the managership of Jock Stein remain unparalleled. While Celtic were continually winning in Europe they were also establishing blanket domination of the domestic scene. The means by which Celtic earned their triumphs was almost as important as the achievements themselves. The manager believed in attacking football and he would send his players out to entertain in a winning way.

Individuals such as Jimmy Johnstone, Bobby Murdoch, Billy McNeill, Tommy Gemmell, Kenny Dalglish and Danny McGrain consistently showed that they were world class performers. Yet such is the special nature of Celtic and their supporters that these men remained extremely close to the club's followers. Stein quietly ensured that would be the case. He himself would go out of his way to express affection for the Celtic support and he consistently displayed a straightforward West of Scotland common sense with which many could identify. His strength of character and ability to bring success to

Celtic went a long way towards establishing a massive modern reputation for the club outside of Scotland.

Stein could be hard on his players but his integrity was such that he could not be accused of any motivation other than attempting to get the best for Celtic Football Club. A glance at Celtic's exceptional League and Cup winning record under Jock Stein shows the virtues of his methods. Jock Stein was a pragmatist but there was also a magic and mystique about his managerial style. Tough, hardened footballers who played under him for years and years talk of the manager's aura and of his charisma. Close analysis of his methods reveals much but it is this unknown quality, this extra dimension, that makes Jock Stein's time at Celtic Park a continually fresh source of fascination.

Jock Stein wears the hoops as he fields questions from Italian journalists in Milan before Celtic's European Cup semi-final with Internazionale in 1972.

Jock Stein (right) takes
to the hills for a
training run with
goalkeeper Johnny
Bonnar during his
days as a Celtic player.

# CHAPTER ONE
# THE MAKING OF A MANAGER

JOCK STEIN WAS BORN INTO COALMINING COUNTRY IN BURNBANK, LANARKSHIRE, ON 6 October 1922. As Stein was uttering some of his first lively cries, equally open-throated roars could be heard at Celtic Park. The day after his birth, a penalty converted by the legendary Patsy Gallacher gave the Scottish League champions a 4–3 win over Partick Thistle. On a foggy afternoon, the Celtic fans went home happy, having seen a first-rate game and their favourites maintain their challenge for the 1922-3 League title.

It was a very different Celtic that Jock Stein joined three decades later. Under the management of Jimmy McGrory, the club had finished the previous season (1950-51) in seventh position in Scotland's top division. They ended their fixtures nineteen points behind champions Hibernian; a massive gap at a time when only two points were awarded for a win. The 1951 Scottish Cup had proved more fruitful – a John McPhail goal in the final had defeated Motherwell. This, however, had been Celtic's first trophy since 1938. By the time Stein joined the club, in December 1951, Celtic were again mid-table in the League and already out of contention for the title.

A solid, well-built centre-half, Stein had spent a decade in footballing obscurity with two clubs. Whilst working as a miner in the Lanarkshire coalfields he had supplemented his income by turning out for perennial strugglers Albion Rovers for eight years. Then, in 1950, he had joined non-League Llanelli of Wales. A year later, a backroom member of the Celtic staff, Jimmy Gribben, had remembered Stein and, at the age of twenty-nine, the player was retrieved from Wales.

'A lot of it was down to him. Not that he was the greatest player in the world, but he was a good captain and a good leader.'

Stein came to Celtic Park chiefly to 'patch', as he described it; ready to provide cover in defence at a time when the club's first-choice central defenders were badly hit by injuries. His signing for the club was heavily overshadowed by Falkirk's £5,000 purchase from Aberdeen of the thirty-seven year old Jimmy Delaney on the same day. The erstwhile Celtic great was now gently winding down his career but his actions still created more interest than the arrival of Stein at Celtic Park.

Four days after joining Celtic, Stein was pitched straight into the injury-hit first team. When his name was announced over the tannoy before kick-off at the match with St Mirren on 8 December 1951, a loud crackle of surprise rustled round the Celtic Park crowd of 20,000. It would not be the last time Stein would be responsible for open-mouthed astonishment at the ground. Stein's craftsmanlike display that afternoon bulked out the Celtic defence and provided his side with the platform from which they sprang to a 2–1 win. A year on, Stein's blend of character and decisiveness saw him made Celtic captain. His leadership and sound defensive skills helped Celtic win the Scottish League and Cup in 1954, the Bhoys' first double win since 1914.

'There was a wee period when Celtic started to win things and to pick up trophies,' says Billy McNeill, later a Celtic captain but a teenager in the 1950s. 'A lot of it was down to him. Not that he was the greatest player in the world, but he was a good captain and a good leader. Those things left a big impression on me, a young Celtic supporter at the time. The fact that he used to knee the ball rather than kick it was quite interesting. He knew his right foot was not the best so he used that leg for kneeing things away. That's not a skill that many people perfect but the big fellow did.'

At the start of the 1955-6 season, in a match against Rangers, Stein jarred his ankle on a rock-hard Ibrox pitch. In those pre-substitute days, injured players were kept on the field as an obstruction to the opposition even if they could not contribute anything else. Stein spent the majority of that August 1955 match limping on the left wing, aggravating the injury as the pain constantly bothered him. Three days later, he hobbled into St Andrews Hall, Glasgow, with his ankle in plaster. He was there to receive the award of 1954-5 Player of the Year from the Celtic supporters. It would be one of his last significant acts as a Celtic player. After several unsuccessful attempts at a comeback, in January 1957 he visited a specialist in London who advised Stein to retire from playing football.

Stein's several jousts with adversity during his playing career had given him a perspective on the game that would serve him well in future years. When dealing with complex footballing conundrums he could draw on a deep well of experience. He had also used the vantage point of central defence, allied to his innate watchfulness, to build up the ability to analyse and read football matches with speed and aplomb. Celtic, recognizing Stein's intelligence and understanding of the game, quickly offered him a non-playing position. That January of 1957, Robert Kelly, Celtic's chairman, told John McPhail, now of the Daily Record: 'We like the Stein influence at Celtic Park and have offered Jock a scouting appointment. He will also learn the managerial side of the business from Mr Jimmy McGrory. This will stand him in good stead for the future.'

Six months later, Jock Stein took a more firm step towards management when he was given control of Celtic's reserve team. Within months he had made his mark. In March 1958 his charges beat Rangers 3–1 at Celtic Park in the first leg of the Scottish Second XI Cup Final. They improved on that performance in the second leg, making their way to a 5–1 win and an 8–2 aggregate victory. More than 40,000 people had seen Celtic's accomplished performances over the two legs. The Celtic team that lifted the Cup at Ibrox was: Haffey, Meechan, Mochan, MacKay, Jack, Conroy, McVittie, Colrain, Conway, Divers, Auld.

'Reserve football was a bit like Junior football at that time,' says John Divers, that side's inside-left. 'It was far better supported than it is now. That Celtic reserve team contained a lot of players who were to be very successful later in their careers but Rangers had a lot of big names playing for them. We were a lot of boys. I do remember

Celtic players await action in May 1954. The previous month had seen Celtic wrap up the double of Scottish Cup and League thanks greatly to the guidance and leadership of captain Jock Stein. Back row, from left: Mike Haughney, Frank Meechan, Andy Bell, Bobby Evans, Bertie Peacock. Front row: John Higgins, Willie Fernie, Jimmy Walsh, Jock Stein, Charlie Tully, Neilly Mochan.

the crowd: there were 22,000 people at Celtic Park to see us win the first game of that final by 3–1. Under floodlights at Ibrox, the Celtic reserves won 5–1 and that was quite a media event – the doings of all these boys, these eighteen and nineteen year olds.'

Stein treated his players with respect, taking a keen personal interest in them. At the time, reserve-team players were almost treated as second-class citizens in comparison to their first-team colleagues. Stein improved conditions, obtaining better training gear for all the players. The reserves had been used to wearing rough woollen fishermen's jerseys for training, which would chafe against their skin. Stein changed that and also ensured that training gear was regularly washed – before Stein's time it had felt to the players as if their gear was washed just once a year. He would sit and talk to the players about the game, taking a genuine interest in them. Occasionally he would discuss tactics but often he would simply speak about people he had met and incidents he had seen during his own career as a player.

'He planted a seed of enthusiasm in everybody at an early stage,' says Billy McNeill, who signed for Celtic, at Stein's insistence, in August 1957. McNeill had played in a schoolboy international against England at Celtic Park that year. After watching the match, Stein had cajoled Robert Kelly into signing the young centre-half. At the time, the chairman, rather than manager Jimmy McGrory, was the biggest influence at the club in terms of deciding which players should be signed.

Soon Stein's accomplishments, highlighted by the newspapers, attracted attention from other clubs. On Sunday 13 March 1960, it was announced that he was leaving Celtic Park to become his own man as manager of Dunfermline Athletic. The East End Park club were second bottom of the Scottish First Division but Stein relished the opportunity. 'It's a great challenge to become a manager,' he said. His first game in charge was against Celtic on 19 March 1960. An injury left Dunfermline with only ten fit men on the field but Stein's injection of spirit saw the Fifers spurt to a 3–2 win.

After Stein's winning start to his full managerial career, Dunfermline pushed their way up the table to finish thirteenth, comfortably clear of relegation and just four points below ninth-placed Celtic. The following season Dunfermline defeated Celtic 2–0 in a replayed Scottish Cup Final to take the first major trophy in their history. Two days prior to the Final, Stein had worked one of his fine psychological ploys, boosting the Dunfermline players by telling them that he had won them a wage increase. In the forty-eight hours before the final the Dunfermline players eagerly signed improved terms for the following season. They could hardly have been in a happier frame of mind for the final.

Under Stein, Dunfermline made their debut in European competition and the manager proved adept at adjusting the team's resources and tactics to the demands of the Cup-Winners' Cup and the Fairs Cup. He also led them to fourth place in the First Division in 1961-2 and to eighth place the following year. Another successful season in 1963-64 would see Dunfermline finish fifth in the First Division. In April 1964, however, Stein moved on to Hibernian, the Edinburgh club's larger support making them a side with greater potential than Dunfermline.

Stein immediately transformed Hibs from mid-table meanderers to championship challengers. By the beginning of 1965 they were two points behind First Division leaders Kilmarnock with a game in hand. 'It's still hard to believe the wonderful change in outlook at Easter Road,' said Hibs captain John Fraser in January 1965. 'You feel it in the dressing

'You feel it in the dressing room, during training, in actual matches. The boss is encouraging and criticizing when necessary. We're one big happy team and going places.'

room, during training, in actual matches. The boss is encouraging and criticizing when necessary. We're one big happy team and going places.'

Celtic, meanwhile, had stumbled blearily into the new year seventh in the League, nine points behind Kilmarnock and out of realistic contention for the title. A 1–0 defeat at Ibrox on New Year's Day had seen Celtic resort to blunt, indisciplined football as they hammered unsuccessfully at the Rangers defence. It was a performance that was not atypical of Celtic at the time. Compounding their problems, Jimmy Johnstone was sent off for a foul on Thor Beck, Rangers' Icelandic forward, and would now face a suspension. Two draws and two defeats followed in the League, leaving Celtic even more hopelessly out of touch with the leading clubs.

The month ended in a more satisfying fashion, when Celtic devoured Aberdeen, beating them 8–0 at Celtic Park, John Hughes scoring five of the goals. The Celtic players' level of performance had been raised by the knowledge that change was about to occur at the club. The following day, 31 January, at a press conference at Celtic Park, Jock Stein was announced as the new Celtic manager. He said: 'Managers are not all that different from players. They must go when the big opportunity comes along. For me, this is it. This is what I have always wanted: a return to Parkhead.'

Stein was the fourth manager in Celtic's history but he would run the playing side of the club in a way that had never been attempted previously. Celtic were about to be dragged swiftly out of the past and into the present. They would then be propelled speedily into a futuristic form of football, the like of which had never before been seen in Britain.

Celtic celebrations outside Hampden Park in April 1954 after the 2-1 Scottish Cup Final victory over Aberdeen. Captain Stein has a secure grip on the cup. His wife Jean and Celtic forward Charlie Tully (left) share the moment.

# CHAPTER TWO
# THE WANDERER RETURNS

CELTIC'S INITIATIVE IN WRESTING STEIN AWAY FROM HIBS PLACED THE GLASGOW CLUB IN A DIFFICULT position. Stein had an agreement with Hibernian that he would remain in place as manager at Easter Road until the Edinburgh club had found a suitable replacement for him. That left Celtic entering the 1965 Scottish Cup without his guidance. Although the 1964-5 League title could be considered a lost cause, the Cup was still very much up for grabs. In Celtic's history, the Scottish Cup had often been the balm that had soothed the end of a difficult season.

First, in February 1965, Celtic negotiated tricky away ties at St Mirren and Queen's Park. Then Kilmarnock, still among the League leaders, were drawn against Celtic in the quarter-final. A sliver of luck fell Celtic's way when they were drawn first, giving them home advantage. With 47,000 in attendance, they squeezed into the semi-finals thanks to a 3–2 win. An identical line-up had been fielded in all three Cup ties: Fallon, Young, Gemmell, Clark, McNeill, Brogan, Chalmers, Murdoch, Hughes, Lennox, Auld.

On the same Saturday afternoon, 6 March 1965, as Celtic were defeating Kilmarnock, Stein's Hibs removed Rangers from the Cup with a 2–1 win at Easter Road. It was the third time Stein's side had beaten the Ibrox club that season and a fine end to his stint as Hibs manager. The following day, Stein was at Green's Playhouse, Glasgow, where 3,500 Celtic supporters had gathered to honour Jimmy McGrory's work as a player and manager at Celtic, a period of honest service that had stretched from the 1920s to the 1960s. Stein joined McGrory on stage on an emotional evening which symbolically marked the end of one era and the beginning of another.

A place was retained for Jimmy McGrory at Celtic Park: he was appointed the club's first Public Relations Officer. As his assistant manager, Stein would have Sean Fallon, one of his Celtic team-mates of the 1950s. Fallon had been groomed by Robert Kelly as McGrory's successor and Kelly had attempted to persuade Stein to have Fallon as joint manager. It was a proposal Stein flatly refused to countenance. He would tackle the job on his own, in his own way, with full responsibility for results and performances. The manager also insisted, upon taking over, that he would have 'full control' of team selection and related playing matters.

Bringing Stein back would have been difficult for Robert Kelly. It was, to some extent, an admission that previous policy had not been entirely successful. The chairman, in the late 1950s and early 1960s, had instigated a thriving youth policy that had brought talented players such as Jimmy Johnstone, Tommy Gemmell, John Hughes, Bobby Murdoch, Bobby Lennox and Stevie Chalmers to the club. During the early 1960s Kelly had attempted to oversee their development with Jimmy McGrory as manager and Sean Fallon as assistant to the manager.

In practice, Robert Kelly would frequently interfere in team selection and would dispense blunt team talks before matches. In the spring of 1964 Celtic had beaten MTK Budapest 3–0 at Celtic Park in the first leg of a European Cup-Winners' Cup semi-final. In the minutes before the second leg in Hungary Robert Kelly had given a team talk. Slapping his glove into his hand, he had told the players that they had beaten this team in Glasgow so they could beat them again here. He imparted no information as to how they should go about their work. Celtic lost 4–0 and missed out on a European final. Kelly's re-employment of Stein was an admission that this managerial 'structure' had failed to work.

Jock Stein, framed by the main entrance at Celtic Park, prepares to get down to business shortly after taking over as manager in 1965.

Robert Kelly, the Celtic chairman whose decision to offer Jock Stein the Celtic manager's job proved a masterstroke. Stein's good relationship with Kelly had developed in the 1950s, during Stein's initial spell at the club.

Kelly had, to a certain extent, had his hand forced. Stein had met the chairman for lunch to discuss an approach from Wolverhampton Wanderers for his managerial talents. When the chairman realized there was a chance that Stein could be moving to England, possibly never to return, he offered him the job at Celtic.

Robert Kelly was also a great believer in tradition. That provided him with an additional agony when deciding whether to offer Stein the job of manager. Jock Stein wasn't a Catholic. Despite Celtic always having been a non-sectarian club, the vast majority of the support was Catholic. The club's directors were all Catholics. All previous managers had been Catholics. After turning matters over in his mind, Kelly came to the logical decision that as Celtic was a football club first and foremost, football should overrule all other considerations when selecting the best man for the job.

When Stein returned to Celtic, many of the players who had known him as their reserve-team coach had become disillusioned by the lack of real leadership on the managerial side of the club. Billy McNeill and Bobby Murdoch were seriously contemplating moving to England. Stein, on his return, put a lot of fun into things. In matches, he didn't try to get people to do things they weren't capable of and he gave the players room for expansion and self-expression. At Hibs and Dunfermline, his work with senior players had added another layer to his experience. His five years away had also allowed him to put a respectful distance between himself and the players he had known during his previous stay at Celtic Park.

Jim Craig turned professional with Celtic in January 1965 and witnessed the beginning of the new regime under Stein. 'He had come up through the mining and there was a hardness about him. Life was hard, being a miner. Anything outside that was, not effeminate or gay, because those words weren't used back then, but cissy-like. We would never get a tracksuit under any circumstances, even on the coldest days. On some days we were not allowed to take our cars up to the Barrowfield training ground. You had to run it, walk it. There was always this element of "Keep them under the cosh". The other thing that people tend to forget is that in 1965, when I went there, National Service had only stopped just a few years before. So the discipline side of that was still there.

'I'd played for Glasgow University before I came up to Celtic Park. We had guys taking us for training at Jordanhill College and they did proper coaching, with balls, and we were doing things like run throughs and exercises with four attackers against three defenders. At Celtic Park they were lapping the track! Suddenly, Jock came in and they started doing things with a ball and all the boys will tell you that suddenly it was very, very interesting.

'At Celtic, before Jock arrived, nobody thought of balancing the back four or getting the various aspects of the team to play with each other. There was none of that. Then Jock came in and started doing this fairly logically. And I think everybody just thought, "This is good. We'll go along with this." I think, to begin with, people just didn't want to be left out because they could see that we might go places with Jock.'

Three days after Jimmy McGrory's gala evening Stein took charge of Celtic's first team for a midweek League visit to Airdrie. The line-up was the same one that had made progress in the Scottish Cup. Ten thousand fans at Broomfield on 10 March 1965 saw John Hughes, at centre-forward, score the first goal of the Stein years. Five further goals, all from Bertie Auld, Celtic's outside-left, followed as Airdrie were brushed aside at Broomfield.

That result helped to entice a crowd of 18,000 along to Celtic Park the following Saturday. The majority of the crowd would hand over their entrance money at the turnstile; season ticket-holders were few and far between in British club football during the mid-1960s. For the League fixture with St Johnstone supporters paid four shillings (20 pence) to enter the ground and five shillings (25p) for the standing enclosure in front of the main stand.

Sitting down at a home match was a luxury afforded to only 4,800 Celtic supporters at each game throughout the 1960s and cost seven shillings (35p). Celtic's spectator accommodation comprised just that one stand, in the southern section of the ground, opposite the boisterous 'Jungle' terracing, which was flanked by two other, vast terraces behind each goal. Apart from the installation of floodlights in the late 1950s, the ground had changed little since the 1920s.

Attendances in the 1960s would fluctuate greatly depending on the perceived attractiveness of each fixture to the public. On Boxing Day 1964, Celtic Park's lowest

The Celtic team in change colours of green top and shorts at Celtic Park in March 1965, the month in which Jock Stein took over as manager at the club. Back row, from left: Ian Young, Tommy Gemmell, John Fallon, John Clark, Billy McNeill, Jim Brogan. Front row: Stevie Chalmers, Bobby Murdoch, John Hughes, Bobby Lennox, Bertie Auld.

Stevie Chalmers congratulates Bertie Auld on netting Celtic's first equalizer in the 1965 Scottish Cup Final against Dunfermline Athletic.

crowd of the season – 9,500 – had watched the home side beat visitors Motherwell 2–0. In contrast, the visit of Rangers in the League that season had attracted 58,000 to the ground while 43,000 Celtic fans had watched the Fairs Cities' Cup second leg with Barcelona in December 1964. Run-of-the mill League games would attract crowds in the low to mid-teens but the midweek win at Airdrie, combined with the appointment of Stein, had added a few thousand to the St Johnstone gate. Some may have parted with their hard-earned cash expecting Stein to turn round the team instantaneously. If so, they were quickly disillusioned. St Johnstone, a side firmly lodged in the lower half of the First Division, left Glasgow with a 1–0 win.

Stein's first modification to the team was as important as any he made in all his years as manager of the club. For Celtic's next fixture, at Dundee, Bobby Murdoch was fielded at right-half instead of inside-right. It meant that the midfielder, whose vision and passing were without parallel, would now play in a deep midfield role, instead of playing just behind the centre-forward. In his new position, Murdoch would have the game spread out in front of him. Using his precise short and long passing he would be able to keep close control on the flow of a game for Celtic.

Jim Brogan, a twenty year old, returned to the reserves to make way for Murdoch in the half-back line. It left one place in the team free. The gap was filled by Jimmy Johnstone, on the right wing. Steve Chalmers moved to inside-right and Celtic immediately looked more balanced. The match at Dens Park saw new confidence coursing through the body of the Celtic team. They were unlucky to return south with only a point after a 3–3 draw.

'What an influence he had on me!' says Jimmy Johnstone. 'I remember playing in a reserve game at Celtic Park against Hibs just after he took over as manager. Nobody knew that Jock had come to the game until he came into the dressing room at half-time. It was the first time I had seen him in there. I then happened to go to the toilet, which is separate from the dressing room.

'Next thing he was standing beside me. "What the hell are you doing here, playing for the reserves?" he said. "You should be in that first team." See, that man for motivation was unbelievable. Nobody had ever said anything like this to me before. "You get out there and show me what you can do," he said. And I went and scored a hat-trick, didn't I? See that wee gee-up, what a difference that made! That was the man's greatest strength. He just knew exactly the right thing to say to every player to get them motivated. Not just with me; with everybody.

'He knew me better than anybody else in the world. He knew all my moods and habits. I don't know how. I think he should have been a doctor – or a psychologist! He knew people and because he knew what made us tick he made us feel we were the best team in the world. He knew how to make us believe in ourselves.'

Two days after the Dundee match, on a Monday evening at Celtic Park, Hibernian, still running on the reserves of energy and self-belief instilled in them by Stein, overwhelmed Celtic 4–2. Observant onlookers would have noticed Stein's running reconstruction of his forward line even as the match progressed. Four of the five forwards had their starting positions switched during the game as Stein worked out his future options.

Five days later, on 27 March 1965, there was no room for experimentation as Celtic faced Motherwell in a Scottish Cup semi-final at Hampden Park. A jittery performance, watched by 52,000, ended in a 2–2 draw. Joe McBride had scored twice for Motherwell and almost got a third with a shot that veered only narrowly wide of the post. Bertie Auld had a goal disallowed for offside for Celtic.

The following Wednesday's replay, watched by a 59,000 Hampden crowd, was a less fraught affair. Celtic buzzed and darted around the field like fireflies in the late-March night. Chalmers, Hughes and Lennox got the goals that gave Celtic a 3–0 win and a place in the final against Dunfermline Athletic. A week later, a 4–0 Celtic win at Easter Road virtually ended Hibs' hopes of the League title. Although the game was an academic exercise for Celtic, the seriousness of Stein's intent was shown by his fielding of Billy McNeill, three days before he was due to captain Scotland in the prestigious Home International with England at Wembley.

Inconsistency, however, had characterized Celtic's 1960s experiences pre-Stein and this would not be rooted out in a matter of weeks. Celtic's next outing, at Falkirk on 14 April 1965, saw a disjointed performance and a 6–2 defeat. Goalkeeper John Fallon had looked ponderous throughout although he had been without the protection of Celtic's solid central defensive duo of McNeill and John Clark, both of whom were injured. The Falkirk result left Celtic fans in a worried condition – the Cup Final with Dunfermline was just ten days away. Falkirk were on course to end the season third bottom of the First Division; Dunfermline would finish third from top. Winning the Final would be no fait accompli.

> 'Next thing he was standing beside me. "What the hell are you doing here, playing for the reserves?"

At Largs, three days before the Cup Final, Stein provided personal practice for John Fallon, firing a succession of close-range shots at the goalkeeper on the training ground. The session over, Stein, in a green tracksuit, slung a bulging bag of balls over his shoulder. He then accompanied trainer Bob Rooney and physiotherapist Jimmy Steele back to the changing rooms. This was a style of management previously unknown to Celtic's players. Jimmy McGrory, in his two decades as manager, had kept a dignified distance from the players and had no part in training them.

Prior to Stein, training routines were basic. Players would lap Celtic Park constantly before being rewarded with a twenty minute game with the ball. Stein realized that in an increasingly sophisticated footballing age, with tactics and man-management to the fore, his presence was required among his players during their weekly preparation for action. Nor did his tactics go over his players' heads. Stein's tactics were simple instructions to his players, telling them exactly what to do as an individual in each upcoming match.

Prior to that Largs training session Stein had named his Scottish Cup Final side: Fallon, Young, Gemmell, Murdoch, McNeill, Clark, Gallagher, Chalmers, Hughes, Lennox , Auld. It was the side that had defeated Motherwell in the replayed semi-final and Hibs 4–0 in the League. Celtic would play 4–3–3. Murdoch would link with Charlie Gallagher and Bertie Auld in midfield. In attack, powerful centre-forward Hughes would be supported on either side by the speedy Steve Chalmers and Bobby Lennox. 'Everybody is now fighting fit,' said Stein on announcing his team. 'From now until the kick-off there will be no hard work at all. Just a few agility exercises and ballwork. The players are tense enough without me having to hammer it home to them every minute. That's why we came down here for a few days.'

Two days before the Final, the Celtic players went home. Those in the side could rest easy, knowing they were starting the match. By kick-off on the Saturday they were fresh, relaxed and ready to push for Celtic's first Scottish Cup since 1954 and first trophy of any sort since the League Cup victory in 1957. A crowd of 108,800 attended, generating record receipts of £36,973, of which Celtic and Dunfermline would each receive £14,397. The vast majority at the match were desperate to see Celtic get their 1960s swinging.

The opening quarter of an hour saw Celtic rolling forward in gung-ho style but they lacked the sharpness of thought to cut through the Dunfermline defence. After quarter of an hour, Dunfermline eased into attack. A high, curling cross troubled Fallon and his punched clearance, under pressure, was ineffectual. When Dunfermline's Jackie Sinclair quickly returned the ball into the penalty area Fallon was grounded. The goalkeeper could only watch helplessly as Harry Melrose pitched the ball into his net to give Dunfermline the lead.

Sixteen minutes later, John Clark pushed the ball to Charlie Gallagher, just inside the Dunfermline half. The midfielder swerved past one opponent to be confronted immediately by another. The Celtic man breached Dunfermline's defensive barrier by striking a clean, twenty-five-yard, left-footed shot. It kissed the face of the Dunfermline crossbar before rising high into the air above the six-yard box. As the ball dropped, Bertie Auld and Dunfermline full-back Callaghan rose to meet it. Once Bertie had decided it was his ball, however, there was only ever going to be one winner. As he nodded in the equalizer, the Celtic end at Hampden exploded into a kaleidoscope of swirling colour. Balloons, scarves and streamers were raised in exultation.

A minute before half-time, a clumsy challenge on Sinclair by Celtic right-back Ian Young, on the edge of the 'D', gave Dunfermline a free-kick. Melrose knocked it to his right and McLaughlin, the Dunfermline centre-forward, sent a low, diagonal shot skidding past Fallon to restore the Fifers' lead. The Celtic defensive wall had broken up with all the discipline of a set of children on the last day of school.

Traditionally, scoring just before the interval is regarded as one of the greatest possible boons in the game. In this instance the goal worked against Dunfermline. Celtic, fired up by Stein's words in the dressing room, now came into their own. In the second half, the potential that had so often been glimpsed in previous years came to the fore. Celtic's half-back line, where Stein had plied his trade a decade before, provided the platform for success. Clark performed a perfect man-marking job on Alex Smith, Dunfermline's most feared forward. McNeill was dominant at centre-half. Murdoch lobbed and rolled his passes all over the pitch in magnificent style. In the forward line, Lennox, as he had been instructed to by Stein, ran hard at Jim McLean, the Dunfermline centre-half, gnawing away at the defender's confidence. The incessant movement of Hughes and Chalmers kept the other Dunfermline backs busy.

With seven minutes of the second half gone, and Celtic occupying the Dunfermline half of the field, left-back Tommy Gemmell nudged the ball away from Dunfermline outside-right Alec Edwards. The ball reached Auld who released Lennox down the left wing. With no Dunfermline player able to get near the Celtic man, he had time to look up and spot Auld racing into an advanced position. When Lennox's swift, low cross reached him, Auld was again the undisputed master of the penalty area. He sent a shot burrowing deep into the Dunfermline net to give Celtic their second equalizer.

Dunfermline were now on their uppers, their only hope was to hold out for a replay and a chance to regroup. But with nine minutes remaining Celtic won a corner on the left wing. As Gallagher placed the ball in the arc, he looked up to see where best he could send it. Since the start of Celtic's Scottish Cup run, Billy McNeill had been practising joining attacks at corners. Now, as he moved forward with serious intent, he made Gallagher's mind up for him. The ball floated into the air, McNeill launched his lean twelve stones at it, and the Dunfermline challenges melted under the intense heat of the Celtic captain's bid for the ball. In one of the most majestic moments of Celtic's history he attained perfect power and direction on the ball to direct it down and into the Dunfermline rigging. On that April night the Cup, and Glasgow, would belong to Jock Stein's Celtic.

Bobby Lennox ducks out of the way as Billy McNeill bores his way through the Dunfermline defence to score the winning goal in the 1965 Scottish Cup Final. Stein saw this victory as being of vital importance. After losing a number of semi-finals and finals in the preceding years, the triumph over Dunfermline encouraged his players to think of themselves as winners again.

# CHAPTER THREE

# CHAMPIONING THE CAUSE

THREE DAYS AFTER THE SCOTTISH CUP FINAL, BILLY MCNEILL WAS NAMED AS SCOTLAND'S PLAYER of the Year for 1965, the first winner of a new award created by the Scottish Football Writers' Association. Against Dunfermline, he and his team-mates had shown that there was natural talent in abundance at Celtic Park. Despite that, Stein was on the lookout for fresh faces. He had visited England in the weeks before the final to check on possible additions to his squad. In early May 1965 he was at Dalymount Park, Dublin, to see the Republic of Ireland face Spain in a friendly international. Stein was there to speak to a continental agent about two possible acquisitions from Spain.

'There are lots of things to consider in this kind of business,' he told Ken Gallacher of the Daily Record. 'We had to know, for instance, how much the player was likely to cost, how much he would be wanting and whether he would like the Scottish climate. We don't ignore any information we get on players of this class. We can't afford to do that.' Stein's interest in the Spaniards would come to nothing although it was sure to have an effect on the players already at Celtic Park. Stein had not specifically identified the players he had watched, or their positions. That would help to add an edge to the Celtic players' appetites for work when they reported back for training in the summer of 1965. The Scottish Cup win was already in the past; under Stein complacency had been abolished.

Spain's summer tour continued with a match at Hampden against Scotland, on 8 May. Again the match would have an impact on Stein. The Scottish team's dismal performance in the 0–0 draw saw the national team manager Ian McColl engulfed by criticism. McColl, under severe pressure from the Scottish Football Association, resigned from his position. The SFA, on 12 May, then announced that Jock Stein would take charge of Scotland for the late-spring World Cup ties with Poland and Finland.

With Scotland's matches against Poland and Finland due on 23 and 27 May Stein had little time in which to prepare for the internationals. The two matches yielded a 1–1 draw with Poland in Chorzow and a 2–1 victory over the Finns in Helsinki. That left Scotland in a decent position in their World Cup qualifying group. Late in the summer of 1965 the SFA asked Celtic if Stein could continue as Scotland caretaker-manager during the 1965-6 season. The Celtic board, after some consideration of the position, agreed to co-operate for the good of the national side.

Celtic and Stein had agreed to the SFA's request only after it had been specified that Stein's duties with Scotland would be confined to supervising the team in the days prior to each international. He would not be required to travel around Scotland and England to keep tabs on the form of Scotland players. In between Scotland's fixtures the manager would devote himself entirely to the Celtic cause. It was an agreement that suited all of the parties concerned, not least Stein. Home and away World Cup matches against Italy early that season would provide the type of challenge he always relished. Sporadic international occasions apart, the manager would concentrate assiduously on restoring Celtic's reputation as Scotland's leading club side.

His international service had not prevented Stein being simultaneously occupied on Celtic's behalf that May. On his return from watching Poland in a friendly international with Bulgaria, Celtic broke the club transfer record with the £22,500 signing of Joe McBride, the Motherwell striker who had caused Stein's defenders a variety of problems in the Scottish Cup semi-final.

The imposing facade at Celtic Park in the 1960s. With Jock Stein in charge as manager at the club, modernization was rapidly gathering pace inside the grand old team's grand old building. Celtic would soon have a team to match the club's history and traditions.

Although the payment for McBride broke Celtic's own record, the club was still operating at a financial level far below that of other large British clubs. The £20,000 transfer barrier had been broken in England two decades previously when Notts County signed Tommy Lawton from Everton. In 1962 Denis Law had joined Manchester United from Torino for a British record fee of £115,000. At Celtic Park neither transfer fees nor wages came close to matching those that were common currency at the top clubs in England. Celtic players were expected to play for the jersey, especially those who had been brought up amongst Celtic-orientated families. The Celtic men of the 1960s were generally happy to follow this tradition.

McBride joined his new team-mates for pre-season training on 19 July, a day on which the longer-serving players were pleasantly surprised. Instead of the traditional, grinding road run that had marked the first day of pre-season work in other years, Stein had the players carrying out ballwork. Every one of Celtic's squad of twenty-eight was given a ball to work with. 'We've been working out some new ideas at training,' said Stein before the 1965-6 season began. 'We've been giving the boys plenty of the ball and letting them work out in squads.

'We place players together in these squads who have approximately the same work capacity and we have the more experienced players as squad leaders. For instance, Billy McNeill, Bertie Auld, Stevie Chalmers and Jim Kennedy all had charge of groups. It gives them a sense of responsibility and I think it also keeps the players working hard.' The Celtic players had previously been trained by being given running, more running and then more running. They found the change of approach thoroughly refreshing.

> 'We place players together in these squads who have approximately the same work capacity and we have the more experienced players as squad leaders'.

Another new ingredient was added to the mix at Celtic Park that summer when Stein arranged for two Brazilians to join the club for an extended trial period: Ayrton Inacio and Marco di Sousa, from the São Paolo club. Celtic would pay their wages and accommodation for one month as Stein sought to expand his horizons. Juan Ramos, the Brazilians' agent, stated: 'If your teams intend to be successful in Europe then they must be ready to bring top-class players from other countries. Celtic, I now know, want that European success and I think they will achieve it.' Di Sousa and Inacio were met at Glasgow Airport on 5 August by Sean Fallon, who drove his car on to the tarmac to collect the players as they disembarked from the plane. He then sped off, with reporters in close pursuit, to take the players to their secret destination. Two other Brazilians, Fernando Consul and Jorge Fara, soon joined their compatriots at Celtic Park.

Celtic players in the mid-1960s had found themselves being criticized for being too well paid and comfortably off. In the press former Celtic stars questioned whether the new generation retained the same feeling for the club that had been prevalent in previous eras. The arrival of supposedly talented foreigners was regarded by some as a much-needed injection of vigour into the Scottish game. Almost every leading Scottish club at the time had at least one Scandinavian on their books. Dunfermline also had a Brazilian on trial while St Mirren had a Guatemalan trialist savouring the exotic delights of Paisley.

Eventually, Celtic would decide against signing the Brazilians. Problems in attaining work permits and the agent's hefty transfer valuation of his charges combined to suppress Stein's and the Celtic board's interest in the signings. Inacio, strangely, would end up signing for Albion Rovers before disappearing from sight. That suggested that Stein's decision not to sign the Brazilians had been correct.

Celtic's 1965-6 season started with an away tie at Dundee United in the League Cup. The tournament at that time was split into eight four-team sections with the winners of each section qualifying for the quarter-finals. Without John Hughes, who was suspended for the first five games of the season, and McBride, missing because of a bruised instep, Celtic lacked a focal point in their forward line and fell victim to a 2–1 defeat. Four days later Celtic produced another stuttering performance against Motherwell, again in the League Cup. The evening was redeemed by Celtic's goal, the only one of the game. Midway through the first half Jimmy Johnstone pushed the ball to inside-forward John Divers, who was positioned close to the goal-line. From the most acute of angles, his swift shot passed between the Motherwell goalkeeper and his near post.

Joe McBride takes to the air in his competitive debut for the club, a League Cup tie with Dundee in August 1965. The centre-forward would net a total of 43 goals in the 1965-6 season. A crowd of 34,000 watched this match at Celtic Park – with Stein at the helm, the fans' expectations of entertainment from their team had swiftly been restored. In 1964-5 the average League attendance at Celtic Park was 20,000. In 1965-6 it jumped to 26,500.

Divers had made more than 200 appearances and had scored 100 goals for Celtic since 1957. Prior to Stein's return to Celtic Park, however, he had lost his place in the Celtic side. 'I hadn't been in the team,' he says. 'I had been injured. And I remember big Jock, being the master psychologist he was, saying to me, when he came back in 1965, "I could never believe it when I picked up the Celtic team and you were not playing. You get yourself fit and you'll be in my team." That was one of the first things he said to me when he came back to Celtic Park. I've heard similar stories from other people. That was a big Jock trait, encouraging people to perform to their optimum for him.'

The following Saturday a stack of chances piled up but weren't taken as Celtic plunged to a 2–0 home defeat by Dundee. The display was initially greeted by a disbelieving silence from the 34,000 Celtic fans present. Stein then found his ears assaulted by a slow handclap as the Celtic fans derided their own players and management. Halfway through the fixtures in their section, and with just two points from a possible six, Celtic looked in serious danger of swift elimination from the League Cup.

It was a relief when, after those three League Cup fixtures, Celtic got the chance to start their season afresh with their opening League match. By coincidence, they started at the same venue as they had begun their League Cup programme: Tannadice, the home of Dundee United. A performance of controlled pace and power left United reeling. Celtic, with goals from Divers, McBride, Young and Gemmell, emerged 4–0 winners. They completed their League Cup section with three wins, scoring nine goals and conceding three, to qualify for the quarter-finals. Celtic's season was now seriously underway.

At Starks Park, Kirkcaldy, on 15 September 1965, Raith Rovers of the Second Division were pulverized 8–1 in Celtic's League Cup quarter-final. Three days later, Celtic visited Ibrox Park for the big Glasgow derby as the only side in the Scottish First Division with

John Hughes (right) leaves the pitch at Dens Park after scoring in the 3-1 League Cup victory over Dundee in September 1965. Joe McBride (left), one of Celtic's other scorers, along with John Divers, follows him. Hughes had been switched from centre-forward to the left wing by Stein and the winger would use his power and pace to score twenty-two goals from his new position in 1965-6.

full points from their League fixtures. With spectators able to roam around the vast Ibrox terraces at will, all sorts of miscreants were able to take cover beneath the cloak of the crowd. This habitually led to trouble at Old Firm matches. The September 1965 fixture saw twenty-one people arrested inside Ibrox for breach of the peace and assault. Thirty others were arrested outside, several of them for attempting to scale walls into the ground after the stand and the terracings were declared full. Again, they knew that once inside they would be able to escape detection in the mobile, unticketed crowd.

The 76,000 who were watching the game saw Stein's first tilt at taking Rangers on their own turf end in narrow failure. The Ibrox men won 2–1 but by the end were hanging on precariously as Celtic pressed them hard. The result saw Celtic slip from first to fourth position in the First Division but they were only a point behind new leaders Hibs.

'The score was 2–1 at half-time,' says John Divers. 'Fairly late in the game we forced a corner-kick at the Rangers end of the park. The ball was crossed and big Billy got up at the point of the six-yard line on the back post and headed it right across the goals. As he started jumping I had started running into the penalty box. About two yards from goal I put my foot up but it never bounced as high as I thought it was going to bounce. It went underneath my foot – I never even touched it. The opportunity was gone and we finished up losing that game 2–1. I never played again for the Celtic Football Club.'

A 4–0 victory over Raith Rovers in the second leg of the League Cup quarter-final and a 7–1 home win over Aberdeen in the League teed Celtic up nicely for Stein's first excursion into Europe with the club. Celtic flew out to Deventer, in Holland, on Sunday

26 September for the away leg of their Cup-Winners' Cup tie with the Go Ahead club. Stein allowed his players to relax gently into their surroundings then arranged for an 8pm training session on the Monday evening, the time arranged for kick-off in the match forty-eight hours later.

A crowd of 25,000 saw Celtic execute Stein's tactics to the letter. For the opening 20 minutes they cagily contained the part-timers' efforts. With Go Ahead's enterprise largely exhausted, fast forwards Bobby Lennox and Stevie Chalmers each prised open the Dutch defence to put Celtic 2–0 ahead at half-time. By the mid-point of the second half Lennox had completed a hat-trick. Jimmy Johnstone collected two goals for himself. With the Celts 6–0 up with twenty minutes remaining they were able to go ahead and indulge in some exhibition stuff, to the delight of an appreciative home crowd. The second leg would prove a formality, Celtic coasting to a 1–0 win.

Following that match in Holland, Stein, Hughes and McNeill travelled directly to Northern Ireland to meet up with the Scottish international squad. After a 3–2 Saturday afternoon defeat in Belfast the Celtic trio returned quickly to Glasgow where their club would face Hibs in the League Cup semi-final at Ibrox on the Monday evening. A 0–0 draw meant the two sides would have to replay the match a fortnight later, on 18 October 1965. This time Celtic raced into a 2–0 lead after twenty minutes and ended the evening 4-0 winners. It put them into the final with Rangers, to be played at Hampden five days later, on 23 October 1965. Stein fielded the same eleven who had won through to the final: Simpson, Young, Gemmell, Murdoch, McNeill, Clark, Johnstone, Gallagher, McBride, Lennox, Hughes.

During the early part of that 1965-6 season, Stein had remained loyal to John Fallon, the goalkeeper who had been the number-one choice on his arrival as manager. After the 2–1 defeat in the League match with Rangers at Ibrox, however, Fallon was dropped. His replacement, Ronnie Simpson, had won FA Cup winners' medals with Newcastle United in 1952 and 1955. He had also represented Great Britain at the 1948 Olympics. After close to a decade with Newcastle he returned to Scotland in 1960, to join Hibernian.

One of Jock Stein's early decisions as Hibs manager had been to place Simpson on the transfer list and, approaching the age of thirty-four, the goalkeeper's days in top-class football appeared to be numbered. It was a surprise, then, when he signed for Celtic in September 1964 for a £4,000 transfer fee. Now he had the belated chance to be on the winning side in a Cup Final for a third time.

A mammoth crowd of 107,600 materialized on the hilly slopes of Hampden that Saturday afternoon. The match, as with all Scottish and League Cup finals in the 1960s, would be televised, but only for the transmission of highlights later that weekend. Television reflected football – football did not reflect the requirements of television. Accordingly, the match would kick off at the traditional hour for all Saturday afternoon fixtures of 3pm. The supporters were there to see whether the balance of power in Glasgow football was about to sway away from Rangers, who had been dominant in the first half of the 1960s. The match provided few long-term clues with regard to that matter although it did clearly establish that Celtic could no longer be considered pushovers.

A sometimes brutal encounter was tilted in Celtic's direction by two penalty kicks inside the opening half-hour. After eighteen minutes, Rangers' centre-half Ron McKinnon launched himself into the air. Under no serious pressure, he clearly handled the ball in full view of even the most precariously balanced individual at the back of Hampden's rough-hewn terraces. Most importantly, his offence was spotted clearly by the referee and, from the penalty spot, John Hughes sent Rangers goalkeeper Ritchie the wrong way.

Ten minutes later, Jimmy Johnstone, enjoying a new lease of life under Stein, had Rangers full-back Provan performing an impromptu twist on the right wing. The Celtic man's mesmerizing close control appeared to have his opponent attempting to move in three directions at once. As Johnstone entered the penalty area, the long-legged Provan lost his balance entirely. Drowning in his own embarrassment, the defender groped at Johnstone as the winger sped past him, pulling him to the ground. The responsibility of taking a second spot-kick again fell to Hughes. This time Ritchie made fleeting contact with the ball as it went past him, sending Celtic into a 2–0 lead.

Celtic kept a strong hold on their advantage. Six minutes from time, an unfortunate own goal by Ian Young gave Rangers a modicum of hope but the afternoon ended with Celtic celebrating their second Cup win in six months, a situation that few among their vast support would have dared dream about a year previously. 'He [Stein] thought that was the result that mattered most,' says John Divers. 'There was the final of a national trophy and Celtic had beaten Rangers. That was a real boost – he thought that was very

The only seating accommodation available at Celtic Park in the 1960s was in the main stand, which had been built in 1929. When Jock Stein arrived at the club, that part of the ground was showing distinct signs of wear and tear. By the end of the decade it would be ready for demolition.

important.' Sadly, the aftermath of the match was spoiled when Rangers supporters ran on to the Hampden turf to attack the Celtic players as they were displaying the trophy to their fans. This incident led to laps of honour being banned at Hampden.

After the League Cup final, Glasgow magistrates ruled that all Celtic–Rangers matches should be all-ticket affairs. Prior to the clubs' third meeting of the season, in the League on 3 January 1966, Celtic secretary Desmond White stated that Celtic Park had been adjudged to have a 78,600 capacity. A fortnight before the match, tickets went on sale, priced at four shillings (20p) for the ground and £1 for the stand. Initially, tickets were released for sale to those attending a mid-December reserve fixture at Celtic Park. They would subsequently be available from the Sportsman's Emporium in St Vincent Street.

Mixed results in Scotland's three World Cup fixtures had seen Stein quitting the post of international team manager in December 1965. A home defeat by Poland had been balanced by a Hampden victory over Italy. The deciding match in Scotland's group had been the return with the Italians in December 1965. In Naples, the Scots had seen their World Cup hopes die in a 3–0 defeat. Frustrated with being hampered in his efforts to run the national team in the same manner as he could at Celtic, Stein quit.

Had Scotland qualified for the 1966 World Cup, Stein would almost certainly have stayed on as team manager but his Scotland duties, in the first half of that 1965-6 season, had done little to drain his enthusiasm for the challenge with Celtic. In November 1965, for example, Stein had flown to Rome to watch Italy defeat Poland 6–1. He had then

flown, via Zurich, to Denmark for the first leg of Celtic's second-round Cup-Winners' Cup tie with Aarhus. He had no sooner touched down than he was supervising an extensive Celtic training session on Danish soil. A 3–0 aggregate victory in that tie took Celtic into the quarter-finals.

In tandem with their smooth progress in European competition, Celtic's League form in the first half of that 1965-6 season had been close to flawless. A 3–1 win over Clyde on New Year's Day 1966 meant that Celtic had won fourteen, drawn one and lost one of their sixteen First Division fixtures. Their tally of twenty-nine points was, however, matched by Rangers. The Ibrox side sat alongside Celtic at the top of the table although Celtic had the advantage of a game in hand. Few Old Firm fixtures have been so cutely poised beforehand as the one scheduled for 3 January 1966.

The Old Firm game had been switched from New Year's Day following the trouble at the League Cup Final. Police appealed for fans to behave themselves, warning that provocative banners and behaviour would lead to arrest. In the event, only four people were 'lifted' inside the ground, an admirable statistic, especially as many of the onlookers had much to be angry about. The 65,000 crowd had anticipated a tight, engaging struggle. They did not see one. After losing a goal in the second minute Celtic powered on to a 5–1 victory. Each goal was a gem on an afternoon when, on a diamond-hard surface, Celtic had mined a host of glittering chances and had taken only the pick of them. It was Celtic's biggest victory over Rangers for a decade and their first New Year win over their Glasgow rivals since 1954.

The on-field success was balanced by things being right off the field. 'Celtic is like one big family,' says Tommy Gemmell, 'and when we used to go to supporters' functions it

Stevie Chalmers watches over the ball as it speeds towards the Rangers net during Celtic's 5-1 pulverization of their Glasgow rivals at New Year 1966. On a rock-hard, rutted surface, Celtic had taken steps to combat the conditions by wearing training shoes. It would be November 1998 before Celtic would equal that scoreline in an Old Firm encounter.

Jimmy Johnstone was twenty years old when Jock Stein returned to Celtic Park as manager. Under Stein's patient guidance, Johnstone became one of world football's most outstanding wingers, with a reputation for excellent unpredictability.

was as if you were members of the family. The rapport we had with the supporters was unbelievable. Big Jock encouraged that. We had a rota system at Celtic Park. Everybody had their dinner dances or supporters' nights or quizzes. And there was always a minimum of three players at each of these functions.

'Now, you start to build up a rapport with these supporters. I always tried to put myself out to get on with them because supporters can be fickle. If you're having a bad time they can get on your back and give you a hard time. They would be a bit easier on me because I was quite popular among them. Additionally, the players were so close it was as if we were related. We used to have parties in each other's houses and go for the odd pint together. And with Celtic being a family club, all these things helped to engender this team spirit.'

Twelve days after the win over Rangers, another powerful performance at Celtic Park, in front of 64,000, gave Celtic a 3–0 first leg win over Dynamo Kiev of the Soviet Union in the Cup-Winners' Cup quarter-final. The second leg, in Tbilisi, involved a 2,500-mile journey via Copenhagen and Moscow. Celtic took 144 eggs, twelve chickens, butter, tea, soup, fruit, fruit juice and steaks with them. The preparations helped them to return with a 1–1 draw and a place in the semi-finals. After going 1–0 down midway through the first half Celtic retaliated in style. Ten minutes before half-time, Hughes guided the ball past three defenders to the by-line. From there, he eased the ball into Tommy Gemmell's path. The full-back, from twenty yards, swiped a shot past Kiev goalkeeper Bannikov.

The return flight was delayed two and a half hours at Tbilisi. After another five-hour delay in Moscow, bad weather saw the Celtic party diverted from Copenhagen to Stockholm, where they were forced to remain overnight. Further technical difficulties with their aircraft meant that Celtic did not arrive back in Glasgow until late on the Friday night. Despite their efforts in representing Scotland in Europe, the Scottish League Management Committee had not seen fit to postpone the Glasgow club's match with

Hearts at Tynecastle the following day. Celtic fell to a 3–2 defeat in that fixture. Four weeks later, a shocking 1–0 defeat at Stirling Albion, then struggling against relegation, saw Celtic lose their lead at the top of the First Division to Rangers.

The travel difficulties the Soviet authorities had imposed on Celtic, the resultant lengthy midweek trip and the loss of precious League points had made Stein temporarily disillusioned with European competition. His outlook had brightened by mid-April 1966 as a relentless roll of winning results had Celtic nicely poised to take the Scottish League title. A 5–0 victory over St Mirren at Celtic Park on 9 April featured Celtic's 100th League goal of the season, scored by Bertie Auld. It left Celtic five points clear of Rangers at the top of the First Division table. The Ibrox side had a game in hand over Celtic but they were fast running out of time – they had only five games left to play before the end of the season.

Tight discipline had helped Celtic to their achievements in Stein's first full season in charge. Stein would have no compunction about carrying out harsh measures if he felt they were required. 'What's up with you?' the manager had asked John Divers in January 1966. The player had failed to work to Stein's requirements. 'I said, "I don't know" because I did not know,' remembers Divers. 'He said to me, "Have you lost a bit of interest in the game?" He gave me a line – clever that. So I said, "Yes, that's it. I've lost a bit of enthusiasm." He then said, "Well if that's the case you're no use to me."'

Divers was made to train on his own between January and March 1966. As the Celtic players headed off to training at Barrowfield, joking and laughing, Divers would be preparing to lap the track or kick a ball around the pitch at Celtic Park on his own. The player trained hard and Stein reintroduced him to the reserves against Partick Thistle in March, where he scored a hat-trick. 'I was starting to lose my hair,' remembers Divers, 'so he was rubbing my head and saying "Alfredo Di Stefano" after the game because I had been playing centre-forward.'

The following morning Divers was injured at training when Willie O'Neill stood on his foot. Divers was out injured from then until the end of the season, at which point he saw a headline in a newspaper announcing that he had been given a surprise free transfer by Celtic. It was the first he knew of his career at the club being over. Once Jock Stein had decided a player was of no further use to Celtic Football Club the end could come shockingly swiftly.

Before the denouement in the League, Celtic fans would enjoy the most spectacular of distractions. Liverpool, League leaders in England, would visit Celtic Park on 14 April for the first leg of the European Cup-Winners' Cup semi-final. A potentially massive club, Liverpool, like Celtic, had slumbered through the 1950s. They also shared a similarity with Celtic in that they had been revived by a single-minded West of Scotland man, in their case the fast-talking, exuberant Bill Shankly. Both men had emerged from a mining background. Stein, serious of intent, nature and expression, gave out his words carefully. Shankly doled them out generously and with a sprinkling of hard humour.

An 80,000 crowd made use of every inch of terracing that Thursday evening. Television viewers would have to wait until late in the night to see the action set down before them in black

By the mid-1960s John Divers, although still only twenty-five, had been a skilful inside-forward for Celtic for close to a decade. Stein had worked with the player in the reserves in the late 1950s and admired his qualities as a clever ball-player. However, when the manager decided he no longer required Divers' services the player's Celtic career came to a sudden end.

Ron Yeats of Liverpool and Billy McNeill of Celtic lead their teams out for the European Cup-Winners' Cup semi-final at Celtic Park in April 1966. Ronnie Simpson, Tommy Gemmell and John Clark follow McNeill on to the field.

and white. Scottish Television would show highlights from 10.38pm to 11.05pm. Viewers could then switch channels to BBC Scotland, where half an hour of highlights would begin at 11.15pm.

Before the game began, Liverpool supporters, packed on the east terracing, spilled over on to the running track. The Liverpool players would also find themselves hemmed into confined spaces. Celtic laid siege to the Liverpool goal, creating numerous scoring chances. Five minutes after half-time, Murdoch bowled to the by-line. From there, he cut the ball across to Lennox. At close range he ripped a hole in Liverpool's blanket defence for the only goal of the game.

Five days later, a 54,000 crowd at Anfield would witness the second bout between the unofficial heavyweight champions of British football. Like Celtic, Liverpool were now poised to take their domestic title, requiring just one point from their remaining games to clinch the prize. The winners of the European tie knew that the final, on 5 May, would take place at Hampden Park; familiar turf for several Liverpool men, as good as having home advantage for Celtic.

Celtic knew they would need a stirring performance in defence and they got one. Simpson, McNeill and Clark formed a hard-edged triangle that frustrated Liverpool for the opening hour. Then Smith's thirty-yard free-kick was deflected and the English side were level on aggregate. Five minutes later, Strong headed Liverpool into the lead. With minutes to go, Lennox slipped through the Liverpool defence and put the ball in the net. When the referee, Josef Hannet of Belgium, signalled for offside, almost certainly incorrectly, Stein knew Celtic were out of Europe. Lennox was exceptionally quick – often his speedy runs would catch officials by surprise, leading to offsides given against him when he had, in fact, paced his pitch for the ball perfectly.

There was no time to indulge in depression: Celtic were due to face Rangers in the Scottish Cup Final the following Saturday, 23 April 1966. A drab affair resulted in a 0–0 draw. The replay saw the Celts swamp the Rangers defence but for the fourth successive match fail to score. A breakaway goal from Rangers' Kai Johansen, twenty minutes from time, gave Rangers the Cup.

In the League, the Glasgow sides were also close to inseparable. When Rangers completed their thirty-fourth and final fixture, they could look at a total of fifty-five points. At that point, Celtic also had fifty-five points but had a better goal difference. They also had one game remaining, at Motherwell, and only a catastrophe could now take their first title for twelve years away from them. A Bobby Lennox goal, a minute from time, provided the perfect topping off ceremony for Celtic's season. The 1–0 win led to the champagne sluicing away down Celtic throats in the Fir Park dressing room as thousands of fans celebrated outside.

'It was all about guidance and leadership,' says Tommy Gemmell of Stein's swift successes. 'The players were there. They just needed to be moulded into a team. And that's basically what he did. We were one big happy family with players that could play. And that makes a big difference. You get a lot of players of good ability in different sides but the actual players don't play as a team. They play as individual units. You've got to get the whole team playing as one single unit before you can get success. And that's what happened with us.

'We thought we could only get better. We knew we had the ability and the players to win the domestic trophies. We were always highly confident – but never over-confident. We also had that little bit of cockiness that you need, to go along with the confidence. Also, we loved playing games. Nowadays, you hear players complaining about the number of games they have to play. We liked nothing better than playing Saturday–Wednesday–Saturday because it meant you did absolutely next to nothing in between except maybe a bit of ballwork, a bit of shooting or a few sprints. You didn't need any heavy training. And players prefer to play rather than train.'

Stein, a teetotaller, revelled in the success, his clear head refreshed by the elixir of victory. Soon he was casting his mind forward to the next challenge. 'It is only in the major European tournaments that you can really get a chance to rate yourself alongside the great teams,' he said. 'Next season we will be in the European Cup for the first time. This is the biggest tournament but I don't think we have anything to be afraid of. The boys have reached the semi-finals of the Cup-Winners' Cup twice and they have had experience in the Fairs Cities Cup. All of that prepares you, gives you the experience you need.'

Regardless of their previous adventures, Celtic were about to enjoy experiences over the next twelve months that would be unique in the club's history.

The Celtic players acknowledge their supporters at Fir Park, Motherwell, after tying up the Scottish League title in May 1966.

# CHAPTER FOUR

# EUROPEAN UNITY

CELTIC HOPED TO BE ENJOYING EXTENSIVE FOREIGN TRAVEL IN THE 1966-7 SEASON AFTER THEIR qualification for the European Cup. It was useful, then, that their close-season tour in the summer of 1966 would make any European journeys look as strenuous as an afternoon drive in the country. Four days after their League triumph at Motherwell, a Celtic party flew out to North America on a long-distance excursion that would see them covering 15,000 miles in total. It was a tight-knit group: eighteen players were accompanied by Jock Stein, Sean Fallon, Robert Kelly and Neil Mochan, the first team coach/trainer.

The players loved nothing better than to have a successful season and then find out they were going to America, frequently the club's destination in the close season during the 1960s. They genuinely enjoyed each other's company and there was a good deal of fun to be had on those trips. For a group of working-class boys it was an amazing experience. They had grown up in the 1950s, with rationing, while their parents had endured the privations of the war and the shortages of the 1930s. Flying to North America for several weeks at their employer's expense was an experience most of their contemporaries could only dream about.

Being away for several weeks also cemented the close relationship between the players and helped them become a successful team unit. Stein, aware of this, did his utmost to ensure the players bonded together, occasionally joining in the fun but at all times maintaining a suitable distance between him and his men. Friendship among his charges would endure throughout their playing days and into the decades beyond.

Whilst on tour that summer Stein learned that he had been voted British Manager of the Year. He was the first recipient of the title, sponsored by Westclox. It was particularly gratifying that the panel of sportswriters making the award was heavily populated by Englishmen. The tour began in Bermuda, where Celtic ran up a 10–1 victory over the Bermudan Football Association and a 7–0 win over Bermuda Young Men. From the island, the Celts flew to New York and then criss-crossed the continent, playing games in Toronto, St Louis, Vancouver and San Francisco.

By the time Celtic met Bayern Munich in San Francisco on 9 June, Stein had only twelve fit players left. Jimmy Johnstone had been given permission to fly home early to Scotland to get married. On the day before he was due to depart, Stein asked him to telephone his fiancée Agnes and tell her to postpone the wedding so that Johnstone could cover for the injured men! The request was politely refused.

The Bayern game, a 2–2 draw, featured a ten-man brawl that sparked off fights between German and Scots fans. At one point Bayern right-back Kunstwadl landed a punch on Stevie Chalmers. Chalmers then chased him over the touchline, looking for revenge. 'Celtic are good footballers but they are primitive,' said Bayern coach Zlatko Cajkowski.

A month and a day after Celtic had left Scotland, a 1–0 win over Atlas of Mexico on 12 June 1966 ended the Scottish champions' 11-game tour. Celtic had won eight matches and drawn three, scored forty-seven goals and conceded six. Although several of their matches had been against local select elevens, the tour had also included three matches with Tottenham Hotspur, of which Celtic had won two and drawn one. 'The trip has been tough,' said Stein, 'but it has strengthened team spirit among the players. We have almost been able to see that spirit grow, especially when we were playing the closing games with only twelve fit men available.'

Jimmy Johnstone (left) and Tommy Gemmell (right) celebrate Celtic reaching the 1967 European Cup Final after the away leg of their semi-final with Dukla Prague in April 1967. On eight previous occasions, British clubs – including Dundee, Hibs and Rangers – had reached the semi-finals and failed to progress. Celtic were the first to make the breakthrough.

Billy McNeill finishes a training session at Celtic Park. The Celtic captain's presence and inspirational qualities spurred Celtic on to several vital victories during the Jock Stein years.

Two-and-a-half months later, on 28 September 1966, Celtic made their European Cup debut with a home tie against FC Zurich of Switzerland. Zurich would be no pushovers: the previous season they had reached the semi-finals before losing to eventual winners Real Madrid. Their coach, Ladislav Kubala, promised his side would play an open game. His players were indeed free and easy . . . when it came to dealing out kicks and punches.

Jimmy Johnstone was the most prominent victim as the Swiss fought furiously and made the most of soft refereeing by Mr Hansen of Denmark. They succeeded in keeping the match scoreless until midway through the second half. Then the 50,000 crowd saw Tommy Gemmell power on to the ball from long distance to score Celtic's first European goal. Stein always encouraged Gemmell to shoot from distance, a tactic that added an extra dimension to his team's attacking shapes.

Five minutes on, Joe McBride got his body over the ball to emulate Gemmell with a shot from distance. That sent the fans home satisfied, but not over-impressed, with a 2–0 win. Too often on the night Celtic had appeared unable to deal satisfactorily with spoiling tactics. A week later, in Zurich, the Swiss, now chasing the game, were forced to adopt a more expansive, less negative style. Kubala, a member of the great Hungarian sides of the 1950s but now forty-one years old, picked himself for his midfield. Having been given the freedom to play football, Celtic celebrated Stein's forty-fourth birthday with a smooth 3–0 win, Gemmell scoring twice, Chalmers once.

'I scored three goals in the two games,' says Gemmell of the Zurich tie. 'I scored a thirty-five yarder at Celtic Park. Believe it or not, I scored an identical goal over there, in Zurich. You would have thought the goalkeeper would have been clued up from the first match. The one in Zurich was from exactly the same distance and at the same angle as at Celtic Park and still he wasn't ready for it. I scored a penalty kick as well.'

Prior to their next European outing, Celtic faced their fourth successive Cup Final under Stein. On 29 October 1966, they met Rangers at Hampden. Nine victories and thirty-two goals had seen Celtic comfortably into the Final, which was watched by a 94,500 crowd. With nineteen minutes gone, Auld propelled a high crossfield ball to the back post. There, a clever reverse header from McBride switched play again and sent the ball zipping invitingly into the centre of the Rangers penalty area. Bobby Lennox flew on to it, sending the ball speeding into the Rangers net before any defenders could react. It was the most stylish move of a hard-fought final and it was all that Celtic required to win their first trophy of the 1966-7 season.

The team's efficiency in the League Cup had been matched by their First Division form. They had started the season with seven straight victories, including a 2–0 win over Rangers at Celtic Park. At the end of October 1966 Celtic were leading the title race, three points clear of second-placed Kilmarnock. Whilst winning in Scotland became a pleasurable habit, European football always promised a taste of the unknown. The Celtic fans now looked ahead eagerly to the next round.

European competitions during the mid-1960s were, to a large degree, unstructured. It was left to the clubs to agree between them convenient dates on which their ties could be played. It was therefore almost two months after their two-legged victory over Zurich that Celtic faced the next stage of their European adventure. Their opponents were Nantes, champions of France, with the first leg to be played in the northern French port on the final day of November 1966.

'I hope the better team will win tomorrow night,' said Robert Kelly at a pre-match reception in Nantes town hall, 'for that team will be Celtic.' The Celtic players mirrored his confidence, stating that they expected to fly back across the channel with a minimum two-goal victory. The Nantes team, which featured nine French internationals, was unlikely to allow such comments to pass without response. After quarter of an hour of the tie, a double lapse in defensive concentration, by Gemmell and McNeill, created an aperture for Magny to poke the ball past Simpson.

Nantes were a fine side but they were soon knocked off their feet as Celtic swept forward. Quick reactions in the penalty box brought goals from McBride, Lennox and Chalmers and a 3–1 win for the Glasgow club. The unpredictable nature and angles of their attacks had produced the predicted scoreline. In the return at Celtic Park on 7 December 1966 Johnstone opened the scoring. He then provided the crosses that gave Chalmers and Lennox the other goals in a 3–1 win that put Celtic into the quarter-finals by a 6–2 aggregate.

Everything remained well under control in the League. A 1–1 draw with Aberdeen at Pittodrie on Christmas Eve 1966, watched by 30,000, saw Celtic celebrate a five-point lead at the top of the First Division. It meant that Celtic had so far gone thirty games unbeaten over the 1966-7 season: sixteen in the League, ten in the League Cup and four in the European Cup.

The only matter to mar the day was an injury sustained by Joe McBride, who slipped on the icy surface and sustained an injury to his knee. He was expected to be out for several weeks – a serious blow as McBride had already amassed an exceptional total of thirty-five goals – eighteen of them in the League – with the season still only halfway through. Providentially, on the eve of the return with Nantes, Stein had signed Willie Wallace, a twenty-six year old forward from Hearts, to add to his squad. He would provide cover for McBride.

Wallace scored in Celtic's next game, away to Dundee United on New Year's Eve, but Celtic lost 3–2, their first defeat in a competitive match since April 1966. They retained their leadership of the League into the spring but were strongly pursued by Rangers. As Celtic travelled to Yugoslavia to play Vojvodina Novi Sad in their European Cup quarter-final first leg on 1 March 1967, their lead at the top of the Scottish First Division had been whittled down to two points. Both Celtic and Rangers had ten games remaining in the League.

In Novi Sad, Celtic matched Vojvodina step for step as the Yugoslavs manouevred the ball around at pace and with clever control. Having spent much of the match countering their opponents, Celtic began to move forward. John Hughes, refreshed after spending much of the season out through injury, cut through the Vojvodina defence only to spin the ball past goal. Bobby Lennox was cut down when clear on goal but Austrian referee Mr Schiller failed to award a foul.

'I feel we have the players fit to wear the mantle of champions of Europe. I have told them so. Now they know it's up to them. I believe our boys and our style are good enough to win this match and win the European Cup.'

As Celtic continued to enjoy their control, Hughes again and Gemmell each came close to squeezing in the opener. With twenty minutes to go, a draw appeared the most probable outcome but a lapse of concentration on the part of Gemmell was followed by John Clark missing the ball entirely. Stanic, Vojvodina's outside-left, beetled into the ominous opening and sent the ball whirring past Simpson for the only goal of the game.

'We all know in our hearts that the European Cup is what counts most,' said Stein before the second leg, at Celtic Park. 'I feel we have the players fit to wear the mantle of champions of Europe. I have told them so. Now they know it's up to them. I believe our boys and our style are good enough to win this match and win the European Cup, with which nothing else compares. If we don't win, well, we'll have to look to the future. But I'm not expecting defeat. We've faith in our play and I think we'll show in this game that we can always bring out something new in football.'

Vujadin Boskov, the Vojvodina coach, was equally confident, stressing that his side would not spend the game defending. It was his stated wish that they would attack. When the match began, however, his players appeared to have made a collective decision to disobey his orders, adopting an entirely defensive strategy. But Boskov displayed not a flicker of dissent on the touchline as his men flipped the ball from one to the other with sanguine skill. They kept possession without showing much ambition to do anything positive with the ball.

By half-time, Celtic had made little progress in finding the key to opening up the Yugoslavs' defence. The howls and jeers of the 75,000 present only appeared to solidify the resolve of Celtic's tough-minded opponents. Then, as the teams took up their positions for the second half, a minor modification showed itself in the Celtic line-up. The usually left-sided John Hughes took up position alongside Jimmy Johnstone on the right wing.

From that moment on, Vojvodina's cool began to crumble as the two wingers rushed at them down one flank, a tactic that even the most assured European defences would have found difficult to deal with. It helped Celtic that their two men contrasted greatly in style. Hughes, 6ft 2in tall and thirteen-and-a-half stones heavy, was expert at employing powerful, skilful runs at a defence. Johnstone, 5ft 4in and nine-and-a-half stones, would pull players out of position with intricate turns, swerves and sudden spurts of pace.

Now, with the Yugoslavs unbalanced by the sudden change in the point of attack, Gemmell swung over a cross from the left wing. Goalkeeper Pantelic fumbled the ball and it fell at Stevie Chalmers' feet. He spurred the ball into the Vojvodina net and the ground exploded in celebration. Pantelic had previously exuded style and confidence and he soon regained his composure after that fifty-eighth minute wobble, dealing competently with Celtic's attacks as the match wound its way towards a close. As the game entered its final minute, a Rotterdam play-off seemed inevitable.

Then Celtic won a corner. Despite the urgency of the situation, Charlie Gallagher appeared unsure of whether to hit the ball short or long. Then time speeded up. A run by Stevie Chalmers drew two Vojvodina men out of their penalty area. It left a gap for Billy McNeill, whom Gallagher had spotted moving into an attacking position. Gallagher curled the ball into the middle of the penalty area and McNeill brushed through a bunch of bodies to get his head to it and guide it high into the net. Uproar followed as the Celtic fans realized that McNeill's leap had taken their team to new heights.

'We said all the time that there were ninety minutes to get the goals we needed,' said Stein. 'We were proved right in the end. This was the finest team we have met in Europe this season and I doubt if we could ever get it tougher. The fans were tremendous. There was some anxiety on the field among the players but there was never any on the terracings. They never lost patience with the team. They simply backed them all the way.'

Stein had rested Johnstone and Chalmers the previous Saturday, when Celtic had travelled to Love Street for a League match with St Mirren. Wallace, who had been signed after the deadline for the European Cup quarter-finals, had played in Paisley but had been ineligible for the Vojvodina match. Reshuffling his side did not present Stein with any major problems. The manager now had cover for every position and was able to reshape his forward line in the event of injuries or for tactical purposes.

'We have a more powerful player pool this season,' he said as he looked forward to the European Cup semi-finals. 'This is what will really make the difference. I will continue to change the team around as often as possible so that no single player will feel the effects of the strain this kind of challenge brings. I am not going to say we will win the European Cup. But there are just three matches and two teams, our semi-final opponents and the final opponents, between us and victory. It is not beyond us.'

Helenio Herrera, the manager of Internazionale of Milan, was also looking forward to his own side's role in the semis. He stated that he wished to avoid Celtic. He regarded them as the strongest of Inter's three possible opponents. 'My idea of the ideal Final,' he said, 'would be Inter and Celtic. And we should beat the Scots on neutral ground in Lisbon in May.'

Herrera's Inter had been European champions in 1964 and 1965 and things appeared to be falling into place for their manager once again when he got his wish of avoiding Celtic. The Italians were drawn against CSKA Sofia of Bulgaria, and Celtic would face Dukla Prague of Czechoslovakia. In the previous round, their experienced side had defeated an Ajax Amsterdam team that contained the nineteen-year-old prodigy Johan Cruyff. Ajax had beaten Liverpool on a 7–3 aggregate earlier in the competition so Dukla's dismissal of the Dutch indicated that they were a side who knew how to go about their business.

The first leg took place in Glasgow on 12 April 1967 and again provided massive excitement for those who stood on the slopes of Celtic Park. Five minutes after kick-off,

Celtic line up in Prague before the second leg of their European Cup semi-final with Dukla. Back row, from left: Jim Craig, Tommy Gemmell, Ronnie Simpson, Bobby Murdoch, Billy McNeill, John Clark. Front row: Jimmy Johnstone, Stevie Chalmers, Bertie Auld, Bobby Lennox, Willie Wallace.

Dukla shuffled the ball through the centre of the Celtic defence with splendid sleight of foot. Outside-right Strunc sprinted through, ready to apply a glossy finish to the move but Simpson was quick off his line to meet the Czech's shot with an athletic, one-handed save. It exhilarated the 75,000 crowd, especially those, like Simpson, in their middle youth.

From there, Celtic's performance had a rejuvenating effect on the crowd. In twenty-seven minutes, Wallace's shot was blocked but bobbled into Jimmy Johnstone's path. Viktor, the Dukla goalkeeper, pounded towards the winger but Johnstone bravely continued his run and lifted the ball over his lunging opponent for a magnificent opening goal. A minute before half-time, Strunc again slipped into space behind a disorganized Celtic defence. This time, he slipped a neat shot past Simpson and low into the corner of the Celtic net. For the second successive European tie, the Celtic crowd would spend the interval in subdued, anxious mood.

Stein, however, had glimpsed weaknesses in the Dukla team. As the second half began, his players pressed their collective playing weight hard against the Dukla back line, turning cracks into chasms. With almost an hour of the match played, Tommy Gemmell, close to the halfway line, sent a high ball swirling over the heads of the Czech defenders. Willie Wallace spun off his markers and poked the ball past Viktor to restore Celtic's lead.

Five minutes later, Celtic's incessant pressure was further rewarded with a free-kick on the edge of the Dukla penalty area. Bertie Auld walked to the ball as if to steady it. He bent over it then, while still leaning down, with characteristic craftiness cleverly tapped it sideways to Wallace. The forward knocked the ball into the net to make it 3–1. The goal, instinctive as it had looked, had actually been pre-planned on the training ground. While Celtic often appeared to be playing off the cuff, everything, except the instinctive workings of Jimmy Johnstone, was the product of Stein's incessant hard work with his players.

A week later, Celtic met Aberdeen at Celtic Park, the Dons having agreed to bring the match forward by three days. Their sporting gesture would leave Celtic with a free weekend before the second leg of their European Cup semi-final in Prague. A 33,000 crowd saw a 0–0 draw on a heavy pitch that left Celtic three points clear of Rangers at the top of the First Division. Both Glasgow sides had three games remaining, one of which was a head to head at Ibrox Park, a match postponed from New Year.

Rested and refreshed, Celtic arrived in Prague on the Sunday afternoon, two days before their match with Dukla. An hour after touchdown in the Czech capital, the players were going through a light training session.

Joe McBride was absent as his knee problem had failed to clear up since he had broken down at Pittodrie on Christmas Eve. In the spring he had been forced to undergo a cartilage operation, but he remained hopeful of returning to the side before the end of the season. However, that looked less and less likely with each passing day. Wallace, despite his leading role in getting goals for Celtic, had not become a straightforward replacement for him. He was still being fielded as an inside-forward, the role for which he had been purchased from Hearts.

It was Stevie Chalmers who now had possession of the centre-forward's shirt. Whereas McBride had been a traditional, muscular, bustling British centre-forward, Chalmers was more stealthy when going about his work, stealing into unguarded spaces in the penalty area and plundering goals like a cat burglar. The return with Dukla would not afford him many opportunities to operate under cover. Stein adopted a 4-5-1 defensive formation that left Chalmers as the sole attacker. As such, his role would involve much scurrying back and forth, harrying defenders and pressurizing them as they tried to build moves from the back.

The match kicked off at 4pm on 25 April in the Juliska Stadium. On the previous day Stein had announced his team, with Lennox and Hughes bracketed in the outside-left position. It was Lennox who got the nod, but neither he nor Johnstone, on the opposite wing, had much chance to show their attacking talents. In defence, Billy McNeill marshalled his fellow backs so successfully that Dukla were limited to only one serious shot, early in the first half. The result was a 0–0 draw that took Stein and his men where no British club had gone before – the European Cup Final.

'Prague was the one and only time we were ever asked to play defensively by Jock Stein,' says Tommy Gemmell. 'We put the shutters up. Stevie played on his own up front and everybody else played at the back of midfield. Ronnie Simpson had a tremendous match, unbelievable. Big Jock, hands up to him, said afterwards, "We'll never play defensively ever again." We had got the result but it was fingernails stuff.

'They never had any clear-cut chances, but they had a lot of half-chances. All it needed was for them to pop one away and they would have hit us like a ton of bricks. We just kept firing balls to the corner flags and Stevie just chased and held it until he got a bit of support. He didn't want to go anywhere or score any goals. We'd hold on to the ball for as long as we could then go back into defence again.

'We all got bevvied on the flight coming back, I think through relief rather than anything else. We had done something that had never been done by any British side before: reach the European Cup Final. So basically the load was off our shoulders.'

In the other semi-final, Inter and CSKA Sofia needed a play-off after both legs of their tie had ended in 1–1 draws. Inter agreed to hand the lion's share of the gate money over to the cash-strapped Eastern Europeans if they would agree to have the play-off in 'neutral' Bologna, Italy. Agreement was reached and Inter duly squeezed into the final with a 1–0 win.

Celtic supporters' minds were already turning to Lisbon. Holiday Enterprises, of Dumbarton Road, Glasgow, were offering five nights' hotel accommodation in the Portuguese capital, together with a ticket for the game. Prices for the trip ranged from £57 to £69. But before the Celtic players could concentrate on the European Cup Final, they had to take care of some important domestic business. Four days after the second leg with Dukla, an unchanged team faced Aberdeen at Hampden Park in the Scottish Cup Final.

Stein still managed to freshen things up within the framework of the team. Jimmy Johnstone was moved from outside- to inside-right, with Stevie Chalmers replacing him on the wing; Wallace took on the role of centre-forward. It was a measure of Stein's controlled confidence that he would use a Scottish Cup Final for one of his little experiments.

Their spirits freed from the burden of deep defensive discipline, Celtic reasserted their self-expression. A crowd of 126,000 saw a goal in each half. Both were crisply-taken shots from Willie Wallace. Each time, a swift run to the by-line had ended with the ball being cut back to the centre-forward, a tactic that left the Aberdeen defenders on the turn and entirely helpless. Celtic had always been in control of the game as they took possession of the second of the major Scottish trophies.

Four days on from the Scottish Cup Final, Celtic faced Dundee United at Celtic Park. A win would see them clinch their second successive Scottish League title. United were rooted in mid-table in the First Division but they were the only Scottish side to have beaten Celtic during the season. A crowd of 44,000 rolled up, expecting to roll away celebrating the first domestic treble in Celtic's history. At half-time, as the Scottish Cup was paraded around the Celtic Park running track, Celtic were 1–0 ahead. The fans fully expected even more exultant trophy celebrations at the end of the match – they had been

Jimmy Johnstone, under intense pressure from Kai Johansen of Rangers, stays steady to usher the ball into the net at Ibrox in the Old Firm match of May 1967. It was the first of two goals on the day from Johnstone that would clinch Celtic's second successive Scottish League title of the 1960s. Willie Wallace is Johnstone's watching team-mate.

promised a lap of honour by the players if Celtic clinched the title on the night. By the mid-point of the second half Celtic had a 2–1 lead and appeared on the verge of victory. Then two pieces of slack defending gave United two goals in three minutes and their second 3–2 win over Celtic in the League that season.

That result meant that the destiny of the Scottish title could now be decided in Celtic's favour in the Old Firm encounter at Ibrox three days later, on 6 May 1967. A draw would take the title to Celtic Park. Helenio Herrera flew into Glasgow in a private jet to catch the match. He had originally planned to wait and see Celtic play Kilmarnock nine days later in order to focus on his own team's crucial championship match with Juventus the day after the Celtic v Rangers game. However, the prospect of seeing Celtic in a match where they would have to give it everything tempted him to Glasgow. The Ibrox stand was sold out before the game but fans of both sides, like Herrera, could make a last-minute decision to go to the game, in their case by paying for admission to Ibrox's vast terraces. On that Saturday afternoon, 78,000 were drawn to the south side of Glasgow.

It proved an engaging struggle. There was even the unusual sight, in the Stein years, of Rangers taking the lead in an Old Firm match. That happened five minutes before half-time but the Rangers fans were quickly silenced. With the tea being prepared in the dressing rooms, a Bobby Lennox shot kissed the post and Jimmy Johnstone was alive to the rebound, depositing the ball in the Rangers net for the equalizer.

Having scored from a matter of inches, Johnstone, as was his wont, then went to the other extreme in the second half. Picking up the ball well outside the Rangers penalty area, he appeared set on one of his involved dribbles with the ball. Instead, he opted for a twenty-yard shot with his left foot that swooped high into the top corner of the Rangers net. It was a magnificently stylish way for Celtic to win the title and, effectively, proved to be the clincher. Rangers did equalize in the dying minutes but the 2–2 draw gave Celtic their second Scottish trophy inside a week. Now all thoughts and resources could be directed towards the European Cup Final, due in a little less than three weeks' time.

Two days before the Old Firm match, Ronnie Simpson had become the second Celtic man to be named Scottish Footballer of the Year. Now thirty-six, the player whose career had been resurrected at Celtic contrasted enormously with the type of opponents Celtic would face in the final of club football's premier competition. The most expensively assembled team in Europe, Inter Milan, counted among their number Luis Suarez, a Spaniard who had cost a world-record fee of £214,000 when he had signed for them from

Barcelona in 1961. Stein was in Turin the day after his side had taken the title, to drink in the strengths and weaknesses of the Italian side. Inter lost 1–0 to Juventus but Stein came away highly impressed.

Ten days before the European Cup Final, on 15 May, Celtic finished their domestic season with a 2–0 win over Kilmarnock at Celtic Park. A 21,000 crowd were treated to the sight of a green-and-white car motoring round the running track at half-time. It carried Scotland's three domestic trophies plus the Glasgow Cup and the Reserve League trophy. It was a collection of silverware that had never previously been garnered by any club. At the end of the match the Celtic players returned to the pitch, carrying Jock Stein shoulder-high.

A week before the final, Herrera visited Lisbon to check on facilities. He returned confident that good public relations work on his part had ensured that the Portuguese would be behind their fellow Latins on the day of the match. Followers of Lisbon side Benfica, however, remembered well the European Cup Final of 1965, played in Milan, when their club had lost 1–0 to Inter in what many of them regarded as dubious circumstances. In the 1960s the suspicion of corruption followed Italian football, and Inter in particular, around like a bad smell.

Herrera's tactics revolved around the use of the libero, a free man in defence. This player gave Inter an extra man when defending. When his side were attacking, he had the versatility to step in at centre-half, left-back or right-back, freeing any of his four fellow defenders to range forward and provide an element of surprise in attack. As a young manager in the early 1960s, Jock Stein had travelled to Milan to study Herrera's methods. His use of overlapping full-backs was a lasting legacy of this visit and was a progressive tactic that most of his fellow Scottish club managers struggled to understand.

Following the Kilmarnock game, played on a Monday night, Celtic spent the rest of the week at Seamill on the Clyde coast. The players trained hard, watched recordings of great matches, played golf and relaxed. Stein took time off that midweek to visit the Café Royal in London. There, for the second successive year, he received the award of British Manager of the Year.

On the weekend before the European Cup Final, the players returned home to their families. They reported to the Barrowfield training ground on the Monday for a light session before flying out to Lisbon on the Tuesday. There, the infectious enthusiasm of the Celtic fans was winning over the locals. Around 10,000 fans from the West of Scotland would be backing the Celts; Inter would have approximately 4,000 followers at the game.

'We will not play our usual defensive game,' he said. 'The Cup Final must be won by scoring goals and we will go after them. I should imagine Celtic think the same way so there should be at least ninety minutes of good, fast, enterprising soccer.'

On the evening of their arrival the players were to be found at the National Stadium, the tree-ringed venue for the final, which was situated to the west of Lisbon. There they trained at 5.30pm, the kick-off time of the match two days later. Stein and his players then returned to their hotel at Estoril.

'When we got to Estoril,' says Billy McNeill, 'the hotel was absolutely magnificent. It was perfect, with a beautiful swimming pool and beautiful gardens. But the big fellow gave you half an hour or so in the swimming pool and then said, "Right, get out of the sun because the sun will tire you." Whether the sun would have tired us or not is another matter. I think what he was doing was always reminding you that you were here to do a job of work.

'It was extreme luxury. So therefore he was showing us, "This is where you are now. You are at the top end of the market. We're here now. But don't lose sight of the reason we're here. We're not here just to relax and enjoy ourselves. We're here to appreciate these luxuries because of the level we're playing at. But we've got here and we'll stay here through hard work and being diligent and remembering that we're here to play a game. He planned everything to perfection.'

Herrera was in expansive mood a week before the match. 'We will not play our usual defensive game,' he said. 'The Cup Final must be won by scoring goals and we will go after them. I should imagine Celtic think the same way so there should be at least ninety minutes of good, fast, enterprising soccer.' Inter's pedigree made them very slight favourites, even with Glasgow bookmakers.

The Italians did, however, have their problems. Sandro Mazzola had been laid up in bed with flu in the approach to the game. He was Inter's leading scorer, with seventeen of their fifty-eight League strikes in the 1966-7 season. On the Sunday before the Final, Suarez, the chief prompter of Inter's attacks, was injured in a vital League game with Fiorentina. The Spaniard had been troubled by injury all season and would now miss the European Cup Final as well as the injured Jair, although Mazzola would be fit. Celtic were still without Joe McBride, who ended the season their leading scorer despite his absence since Christmas Eve.

'This will be a very difficult game,' said a troubled Herrera. 'Inter will not be able to count on two of their best players – Suarez and Jair – but the greatest obstacle will be Celtic.' Stein commented in the approach to the match: 'Variety of style is the number-one priority in modern football. You must be able to vary your play to change pace, to switch players.'

'It was Ascension Thursday so a lot of us went to Mass first,' Jim Craig remembers of the morning of 25 May 1967. 'Then we had a wee, light session in the grounds of the hotel. Jock was great at keeping the focus on the game but relaxed as well. Hard sessions would suddenly be interspersed with a bit of fun. You'd maybe be doing shooting practice and then it would stop and you would have a game of rounders. Then you would go back into something quite serious again. Or he would pick somebody and they would be the butt for the day. That was just a way of making things different because there's only so much you can do every day.'

Twenty-one nations across Europe tuned into the game. Across Britain, the match was transmitted 'live' by the BBC. The prestigious nature of the occasion was marked by Kenneth Wolstenholme, the BBC's top football commentator, being given the task of describing the action. He would describe the unfolding events in his usual refined style. The BBC's broadcast began at 5.20pm. At half-time there were fifteen minutes of news – in the 1960s the public had to get by without the opinions of 'panels of experts'. STV also broadcast the match, as did Grampian.

Billy McNeill led the team from the dressing room, up a flight of steps and into the glinting sunlight of the National Stadium, with Bobby Murdoch bringing up the rear. Stein followed his men. Looking cool and confident in dark suit and shades, Stein could have had a lead role in La Dolce Vita. Now his players also had to show themselves the equals of Inter in terms of sophistication.

The following Celts started the game: Simpson, Craig, Gemmell, Murdoch, McNeill, Clark, Johnstone, Wallace, Chalmers, Lennox, Auld. Four others had played their part in getting Celtic to the Final. Willie O'Neill had been left-back for the ties with Zurich and Nantes. From the quarter-finals onwards he had been displaced by Jim Craig whose athleticism made him vastly superior as an overlapping full-back. Gemmell had then returned to left-back to make way for Craig on the right. Joe McBride, who had played in the matches at home to Zurich and away to Nantes, was injured. Charlie Gallagher had been used by Stein as a midfield option in the home ties with Nantes and Vojvodina.

The most unlucky of the four was John Hughes, who had played in five of the previous eight games and who had missed the Nantes matches only through injury. A severely poisoned ankle meant he would miss the Lisbon match. 'As it happens I was unfit,' he says, 'but I wouldn't have played anyway. When it came to the first leg against Dukla he [Jock Stein] was dithering between Bobby Lennox and myself, and he played me. It was a dry, windy night, the park was bumpy and the wee full-back I was playing against was lightning quick. I had a nightmare, I just didn't play well at all. And that was it. He dropped me and I knew that I wouldn't be playing in the Final. And that was down to me. It's my biggest regret.

'He played Bobby Lennox in the return with Dukla and in the Final. As it happened, in between I played in a League game, I got a kick on my ankle and it got poisoned. I went to the European Cup Final but spent almost the entire time in Lisbon in my bed because the journey by air had aggravated the injury. Even after the game I didn't feel part of it because I hadn't been involved.'

Inter kicked off but were quickly dispossessed and Celtic began as they meant to continue, setting Johnstone free on the right wing to attack the Italian defence. It was, however, Inter who created the first clear chance, centre-forward Sandro Mazzola stooping for a close-range diving header in the third minute. Simpson made an impressive reflex save. Two minutes later, Inter goalkeeper Giuliano Sarti, playing in his fourth European Cup final in ten years, was equally impressive. He swooped low to his left to hold a low, left-footed shot from Jimmy Johnstone.

Sarti quickly excelled again, stretching backwards to tip a Johnstone header over the bar. When Inter cleared the corner, they swiftly got the ball forward to Mazzola who began probing the Celtic defence, which fell back in retreat. Spotting an opening, the Italian whisked a clever, diagonal ball into the Celtic penalty area for his fellow forward Capellini to chase. As the wide attacker moved on to it, Jim Craig, who had followed his opponent's run from left to right, made contact with him. The Inter player rolled over four times and referee Kurt Tschenscher of West Germany awarded a penalty. Mazzola stroked the ball low into the left-hand corner of Simpson's net and Celtic had the start they had dreaded: 1–0 behind to the Italian masters of defence in depth. Just seven minutes of the match had been played.

'I don't think it was a penalty,' says Jim Craig. 'I knew he was a left-footed player and I knew that as he went down

Bobby Lennox concentrates on a cross during the first half of the 1967 European Cup Final in Lisbon's National Stadium. Under intense heat, the Celtic players maintained an exceptional work-rate from start to finish of the match.

that inside-right channel he would try and pull the back on to his left. I was merely making sure that if he did that he would bump into me. He collided with me. I didn't tackle him or anything like that. I just angled my run so that the two of us would bump into each other. Very few referees would have given a penalty for that seven minutes into the European Cup Final.

'Their whole aim was to instil catenaccio into the game and when they went one-up a few of them went further back again. In many ways they played into our hands because they gave us the chance to build up momentum. It was a hard day and it involved a lot of work. Gemmell and I worked very hard that day. Giving away the penalty was, in the end, a fortunate thing because it gave us carte blanche to come forward whenever we wanted to. My father wasn't very happy about it. He'd come all that way only to see me giving away a penalty!'

Inter did not immediately retreat into defence. After the goal they continued to push the ball forward, looking for the killer second. This didn't last long. With Celtic stung into a hugely positive attacking response, the Italians were soon forced into getting behind the ball at every opportunity. Whenever a Celtic defender won the ball they would immediately force it forward. Inter were not used to this. In the Italian League, teams would tend to pressurize each other heavily only when the ball was in the final third of the field. Now Inter found themselves facing a Celtic team who were rushing their opponents into mistakes in all areas of the pitch. Inter were hustled out of their usually certain stride. Having disturbed their opponents' equilibrium, the Celtic midfielders and attackers were soon cutting great swathes through the Inter defence.

With eleven minutes gone, Bertie Auld stole some space on the left-hand side of the Inter penalty area and swivelled on to a shot that rebounded from the crossbar. Within a minute, a Lennox snapshot from twenty yards was heading for the roof of the Inter net. Sarti rose to the occasion yet again, holding the ball confidently above his head. By the middle of the half, Inter had settled into catenaccio and, to some extent, it appeared to be working. For a spell, Celtic's attacks became a trifle more hurried, less sustained, more sporadic. It appeared as though Inter might have ridden out the post-goal storm but with every breach of their back line the fabled Milanese resistance was gradually being worn down.

Ten minutes before half-time, a curling volley from Gemmell forced Sarti to stretch low to his left, tipping the ball round his post at the last possible moment. Five minutes on, Inter threatened the Celtic goal for the first time since their penalty, as a low, twenty-yard shot from Mazzola was saved comfortably by Simpson. A subsequent Inter attack was broken up by Simpson with some panache. As the Inter forward Capellini chased a long ball through the middle the Celtic goalkeeper ran from goal and audaciously backheeled the ball away.

'It was sickening at the time to lose the penalty,' says Billy McNeill, 'but it meant that we had no option but to push forward. At half-time it took big Jock a bit of time to settle us down because we were all having a go at the referee, giving him pelters. It took him time to calm us, which he did do and, of course, we went out and it all went right. He encouraged us to keep doing what we had been doing in the first half.'

The second half had barely begun when Celtic were awarded an indirect free-kick inside the Inter penalty area. It resulted in a shot from Gemmell which penetrated the Inter defensive wall before striking the foot of Picchi and spinning goalwards. Sarti streaked after it and, at the last, plummeted to earth to hold the ball on the line. A Celtic goal appeared to be creeping ever closer.

'I didn't have a particularly good game in the European Cup Final,' says Jimmy

Johnstone, 'simply because it was a hard, tense game and it was difficult to play against their man-to-man marking. We did our bit but the people who really excelled there were the midfield and the full-backs. We had to take people here and there to take people out of position and give the full-backs space.'

One of those full-backs, Gemmell, became the only player to be booked during the match after he had committed a foul on the left wing. In the sixty-third minute, he was involved more positively. Murdoch spread the ball from left to right, finding Jim Craig on the overlap and on the edge of the Inter penalty area. Craig nudged the ball forward as five Inter defenders scurried across to cover the yawning gap that had been exposed in their defence. Swiftly, Craig again reversed the angle of play by placing a crisp cut-back into the path of Gemmell. Running at considerable speed, the left-back made an immaculate first-time connection with the ball as he reached the edge of the penalty area to batter it high into the roof of the Inter net.

Celtic's commitment to all-out attack had been shown by Stein's two overlapping full-backs combining for the goal. 'I think Jock always had this idea that he wanted his full-backs to come forward,' says Jim Craig. 'I'd always overlapped – I'd always got a row at school for doing so, even when I was playing at centre-half. It was something I continued to do when I went to Celtic Park. Gemmell was always happy to attack a wee bit as well. Don't forget, full-backs traditionally didn't get the ball very much so if you got it you weren't going to give it away to someone!

'While the full-backs were free to go forward, John Clark would stay back throughout a match and Billy would, more or less, also stay back all the time. Overlapping was a wee bit primitive in Jock's early days because we were expected to get forward and also get back as well, which is a long run. You'd be doing eighty yards down the park and eighty yards back – and the old knees are going. It then became a bit more organized as time went on. Murdoch would step back into the right-back role or the wing-back role as they would call it now. Then I could stay up the park a wee bit more. But to begin with, it was an extremely long run.'

Inter goalkeeper Sarti scoops up the ball as he and his five fellow defenders attempt to control a rampant Celtic side during the second half of the Final in Lisbon. On this occasion, Bobby Murdoch is the thwarted Celt. Murdoch and fellow midfielder Bertie Auld opened up huge amounts of space in the Inter midfield. Their passing prowess, allied to the width offered by overlapping full-backs Jim Craig and Tommy Gemmell were key elements in Celtic's victory.

Stevie Chalmers turns away in triumph after steering the ball past a startled Giuliano Sarti for the second goal in Celtic's 2-1 European Cup Final victory. Tommy Gemmell and Willie Wallace look on. The National Stadium, Lisbon, was an unusual venue for a European Cup Final. Three sides of the ground towered over the pitch; the other side housed a tiny stand of a similar size to those found at the homes of the smaller Scottish Second Division clubs.

Inter had been wilting prior to the goal. Now their defence began to melt under the heat of Celtic's sustained pressure. The action continued to be concentrated in and around the Inter penalty area and only the excellence of Sarti prevented Celtic getting a swift second.

With five minutes remaining, Gemmell was allowed time and space to run on to a pass on the left wing. Emulating Craig at Celtic's first goal, the left-back hovered over the ball, drawing defenders to him. He then turned it back into the path of Murdoch on the edge of the area. The midfielder's first-time shot sped across the face of goal. On the edge of the six-yard box, Chalmers extended a boot to turn the ball into the net. As simply as that, Celtic had their precious winning goal. It was classic Celtic: simple in its execution but created by much hard work and exquisite movement in the previous eighty-five minutes.

'When they got the early goal,' says Billy McNeill, 'I think they underestimated the skill and the quality we had in the side. We had players such as Jimmy who could destroy anybody. Stevie Chalmers and Bobby Lennox and Willie Wallace were persistent, sharp and runners. Wee Bertie was a great passer of the ball. Murdoch could pass it, strike it and score. He could do the lot. Tommy Gemmell and Jim Craig could go up and down either side all day long. I don't think Inter expected the amount of creativity that was in the side. It took us a long time to break them down and that is testimony to how good they were.

'They also carried a lot of luck: 2–1 was not a real reflection of the way the game had gone. For myself and John Clark, after they scored, it was probably the easiest game we had in the competition. They were an excellent side – they had some fabulous players but by the time the second goal went in they had just given up. They had just accepted second best.'

'Billy was brilliant in the air,' adds Jim Craig, 'and really just cleared his lines on the deck. He very seldom did anything of a distributive nature. He would just pass it to Murdoch, Gemmell, myself or Clark and it would be passed on from there. Without Jock, none of it would have happened. You cannot be more clear than that. If he hadn't come back in 1965 quite a number of players who two years later were European champions would have left. We just wouldn't have won the European Cup. We were literally going nowhere. Even guys like Neilly Mochan, behind the scenes, were saying that the club was on a downhill slope.'

At Glasgow Airport, the twenty-strong Celtic party was greeted by Lord Provost John Johnston and John Lawrence, the owner of Glasgow Rangers. Stein had appealed to the fans not to go to the airport but to turn up for a victory parade at Celtic Park instead. Celtic had become the first team in football to win their domestic League and Cup in the same season as winning the European Cup. There was no doubt, however, as to which trophy was the most valuable of the three. Celtic, with the finest Scottish sporting performance of the twentieth century, had become only the fifth team who could claim the privilege of calling themselves champions of Europe. Their feat elevated their name to stand alongside Real Madrid, Benfica, AC Milan and Inter Milan, the previous winners of the tournament. Equally importantly, Celtic had won the trophy in the fashion that Frenchman Gabriel Hanot had desired when he had founded the European Cup in the mid-1950s. Celtic had done everything required of them and they had done it in style.

The Celtic players enjoy a lap of honour at a packed Celtic Park twenty-four hours after their magnificent triumph in Portugal. The European Cup is held up for all to see as the players burst into Celtic song.

# CHAPTER FIVE

# LIFE WITH THE LIONS

THE TRIUMPH IN LISBON ENSURED THAT A CASCADE OF ACTIVITY WOULD SURROUND CELTIC IN THE ensuing months. The players were given a week's rest after the European Cup Final before training for the special honour of providing the opposition in a testimonial match for Alfredo Di Stefano of Real Madrid on 7 June 1967. Di Stefano, the magnificent Argentinian forward, and his Real Madrid team-mates had created the original hallmark of style that had made the European Cup special. They had won the trophy five successive times between 1956 and 1960. Those excellent wins had established the tournament as a credible supplement to domestic competition and had won Real admirers from all parts of Europe.

Jock Stein was one such admirer. He had been present at Hampden Park for Real's crowning glory. In the greatest of those first five European Cup finals, in the spring of 1960, he and 127,000 others had marvelled at their 7–3 win over Eintracht Frankfurt. The panache with which Real achieved that victory had inspired him to try and emulate them. In the Bernabeu Stadium, Madrid, seven years later, he looked on as his team put into action the type of principles that Real had established for true champions of Europe.

Celtic's sophistication left Real, who had been European Cup winners in 1966, looking rustic in comparison. The Glasgow team won 1–0 and Jimmy Johnstone produced what he considers to be his finest performance as a footballer. By the closing minutes of the match, Spanish defenders were turning their backs on Johnstone rather than taking him on; he had mesmerized them once too often on the evening.

'He never asked you to do something you weren't capable of doing,' says Tommy Gemmell of Stein. 'He had a great saying: "Play to your strengths and disguise your weaknesses." He made us very tactically aware, we were extremely fit, he was good at motivating. He was always experimenting – he tried a lot of things in training that sometimes we would never use in matches because he thought they wouldn't work. Everyone played to their strengths.'

With his team indisputably number one in Europe, Stein had, after the final against Inter, immediately begun looking for new worlds to conquer. Barely had the players caught their breath after the exhilaration of Lisbon than Stein was looking ahead to the World Clubs Cup, a trophy contested between the champions of Europe and the champions of South America. 'Whoever we have to play from South America, we shall attack,' he said in the hours after despatching Inter's catenaccio to the dustbin of footballing history. 'We want to show South America, as well as Europe, that defensive soccer is finished.'

Their opponents in that home-and-away contest were Racing Club of Buenos Aires. Before that momentous meeting, however, Celtic began their defence of the European Cup. Their first steps in that direction led them only as far as their first home defeat in European competition. At Celtic Park, in September 1967, they lost 2–1 to Dynamo Kiev. Tickets for the second leg in the Ukraine sold for as much as £15 for a ticket although they only had a £1 face value. After an hour of the match, Celtic's immediate European Cup future became cloaked in gloom. Bobby Murdoch was sent off for throwing the ball away in disgust after a foul that had been awarded against him by referee Mr Sbardella of Italy.

Instead of depressing Celtic, that incident released them into effusive inventiveness. Two minutes later, Bertie Auld sent a free-kick into Bobby Lennox's path and the forward

Joe McBride sweats his way round the Celtic Park pitch in the summer of 1967 in an attempt to regain fitness for the new season. Sadly for McBride, he would fail to regain a regular place in the Celtic team after the cartilage trouble that had disrupted his career.

caressed a shot past goalkeeper Bannikov from the sharpest of angles. Celtic made another quick deposit in the Kiev net when John Hughes, fielded at outside-right by Stein, made tracks through the middle and pushed the ball between Bannikov's legs. Sbardella disallowed the goal although no offence was apparent.

As the seconds ticked away, an aggregate draw looked certain. Then Byshovets, the Kiev outside-right, slipped into space to score the equalizer on the night and win the tie for Kiev. Celtic, who had achieved so many positive firsts the previous season, thus became the first defending champions to be knocked out in the first round of the European Cup. 'The referee was "got at", definitely,' says Jimmy Johnstone. 'He denied us two goals and a penalty.'

'Now,' said Stein on his return from the Soviet Union, 'we must concentrate all our efforts on two things – the winning of the World championship and the League championship.' A fortnight later, on 18 October 1967, Racing Club were at Hampden Park for the first leg of the World Clubs Cup. The match had been moved to Scotland's national stadium to accommodate an extra-large crowd of 103,000. They were drawn to see whether Celtic could emulate Real Madrid and Internazionale, who had been the only European sides to win the title of club champions of the world since the trophy's inception in 1960.

Senor Bizzuti, the Racing Club coach, said before the match: 'We know that Celtic are very fast but there is no point in being fast if you do not have the ball. It will be our plan to prevent Celtic getting it.' His side's means of carrying out his plan were soon revealed. Celtic's first effective attack ended with Jimmy Johnstone being hauled to the ground by Racing centre-back Basile on the fringes of the eighteen-yard box. Spanish referee Mr Gardeazabal awarded a free-kick to Celtic outside the area. That set the tone for an evening when Argentinian gamesmanship would dance an unattractive tango with overly lenient Spanish refereeing.

As the Argentinians hacked away at the Celtic players – most often Johnstone – Celtic were hustled out of their stride. When chances fell to the feet of Celtic men, their resultant lack of rhythm led to misplaced shots. It took Billy McNeill's unquenchable spirit to salvage some satisfaction from the game. Shortly after half-time, he knocked a header against the Racing post. Then, with twenty minutes to go, Hughes' corner dropped out of the night sky and McNeill brightened Celtic faces around the ground with a header that looped over Racing's defenders and into the net. It was the only goal of the game.

Ten days later, Celtic were back at Hampden to face Dundee in the League Cup Final. Celtic were aiming to become the first club to win the League Cup in three successive seasons. Watched by a crowd of 66,660 they settled the match with five goals neatly interspersed at even intervals in a 5–3 win. After going ahead with their first goal, through Chalmers after six minutes, Celtic never lost the lead and were never in any danger of relinquishing the trophy.

Later that Saturday evening, an eighteen-man playing squad flew out to Buenos Aires. One hundred Celtic fans paid £200 each to accompany the team – a price that included the flight, accommodation in Argentina and an extension to their stay if the tie required a play-off in Montevideo, Uruguay. After a twenty-hour journey, the Celtic players were shuttled from Buenos Aires Airport to the Hindu club, twenty miles north of the city.

Jimmy Johnstone is grounded after one of numerous fouls perpetrated on him by the players of Racing Club in the first leg of the World Clubs Cup Final at Hampden Park in October 1967.

The second leg of the 1967 World Clubs Cup, on 1 November, degenerated into chaos even before a ball was kicked. As the teams warmed up, Ronnie Simpson was struck on the head by a missile. He had to be replaced by John Fallon. The Celtic players found it difficult to believe the missile had been thrown from the crowd. A wire mesh behind the goal was in place to protect the players from such a danger. It seemed more likely that someone closer to the action, such as a photographer or an accredited official, might have launched the attack. After the withdrawal of Simpson, the Celtic players' renewed attempts to focus on the coming ninety minutes were again troubled when Stevie Chalmers picked up a knife that had been thrown on to the field of play.

The aggravation continued after kick-off as Racing pushed, pulled and pummelled the Celtic players all over the pitch. Midway through the first half, however, Cejas fouled Johnstone inside the penalty area. Mr Marinho, the Uruguayan referee, showed admirable resolve in awarding a penalty. Tommy Gemmell stepped up and, in his usual style, thumped the ball powerfully into the centre of the net. The lead should have set Celtic up to control the match: Stein had drafted in Willie O'Neill in place of Hughes to give Celtic an extra man in midfield and a more compact 4–3–3 formation. However, in the thirty-third minute, Maschio crossed and Raffo lobbed a header over Fallon for the equalizer. Four minutes after half-time, Rulli's through-ball was met by Cardenas and his low, controlled shot raced past Fallon to make it 2–1 to the Argentinians.

The scoring ended there. Away goals did not count double and penalty shoot-outs had yet to be invented. There would be a play-off in Montevideo three days later. Stein commented: 'We don't want to go to Montevideo or anywhere else in South America for a third game but we know we have to.' The Celtic manager remained visibly furious in the aftermath of the game. 'It was terrible, terrible,' he said. 'I would not bring a team back here for all the money in the world.'

John Hughes remembers: 'The game at Hampden was rough and the second game was terrible as well; I think they got a goal that was suspiciously offside. Bob Kelly wanted to come home. He said, "If they want it as badly as that then let them have it." Big Jock wouldn't hear of it. He wanted to be the first British manager to win the World Clubs Cup.'

For three days a tense Celtic party awaited the play-off. Their uneasiness was reinforced as the play-off began. The Racing players, for the third successive time, concentrated much of their resources on stamping an unlawful authority on the game. Celtic players were yet again spat upon and treated to a succession of vicious, niggling fouls. Stein had said beforehand that Celtic would win because they were the better team. They were not given the chance to prove it. The referee, Mr Osorio of Paraguay, failed to uphold the laws of the game.

Provoked once again, the Celtic players' patience finally snapped. Ten minutes before half-time, Johnstone suffered the latest in a series of fouls on him, this time carried out by Rulli. Osorio was immediately surrounded by Racing players as they attempted to create a smokescreen to cloud the referee's thoughts. Celtic players were dragged into the fray.

Bertie Auld lays hands on Maschio of Racing after a nasty foul by the latter during the play-off for the World Clubs Cup in Montevideo, Uruguay, in November 1967.

When matters died down, Lennox and Basile were dismissed; Lennox in a clear case of mistaken identity. Any confidence Celtic had in the referee instantly disappeared.

Three minutes after half-time, Johnstone hit out when Racing defender Martin aimed a kick at him. The Scot was dismissed. Eight minutes later Cardenas beat Fallon with a long-range shot to put Racing 1–0 ahead. With fifteen minutes to go, Hughes was sent off for trying to kick Cejas, the Racing goalkeeper. Rulli was then sent off for punching Clark, leaving nine Argentinians to face eight Scots.

The game now resembled a running street battle and two minutes from time Uruguayan riot police, armed with swords, took to the field in an attempt to restore order. Instead, further chaos ensued when Osorio attempted to dismiss Auld only to find that the Celtic midfielder refused to leave the pitch. The referee, his authority entirely undermined, had little option but to allow the final minutes to be played out with a player he had dismissed still on the field of play. As Celtic arrived back at Prestwick Airport at 11pm on Monday 6 November, half an hour of World Clubs Cup 'highlights' were being broadcast across Britain. Kenneth Wolstenholme described the show as 'the Battle of the River Plate'.

The Celtic players were given two days off and Celtic directors stated that they would be making no comment on the situation until after a board meeting. Out of this silence arose rumours that Stein had been sacked or was resigning as Celtic manager. On 9 November the board met. Robert Kelly announced afterwards: 'A reason for our players forgetting themselves and losing their tempers so badly was the fact that Johnstone, who had been so badly abused in all three games, was most unfairly dismissed by the referee. Having said that, we come to the fact of what Celtic FC are going to do about this. We are in this together, from the chairman to the players. We feel that for our reputation and also for the reputation of football, the players must suffer for their conduct. We do not want to individualize and we are taking the unprecedented step of fining the whole team £250 per player.'

After their ballistic intercontinental affair, Celtic fell back to earth on 11 November with a visit to Airdrie, coming away with a 2–0 win. Scottish mud and homely stands must never have looked so good as on that Saturday afternoon. At that point in the 1967-8 League season, Celtic were five points behind leaders Rangers but with two games in hand. For Celtic, the rest of the season, in contrast to its opening weeks, would contain few distractions from the task of winning a third championship in succession. Their first outing in the 1968 Scottish Cup ended in defeat by Dunfermline. It was the first time in seven domestic cup campaigns under Stein that Celtic had failed to reach a final.

In the League Rangers once again proved to be Celtic's closest challengers. In mid-April 1968, as a taut title race reached its climax, Celtic beat Dundee 5–2 at Celtic Park to take their tally of League goals to 102. It left the Celtic Park club one point ahead of Rangers with two games to play. This time, however, Rangers, ominously, had one game in hand. On Wednesday 17 April, as Celtic faced Clyde in the minor distraction of the Glasgow Cup Final at Hampden, Rangers were fulfilling their spare League fixture, at Morton. As Celtic went full steam ahead for an 8–0 win, the majority of the 25,000 crowd greeted with delirious cheering the news from Cappielow that Morton had held Rangers to a 3–3 draw. It left Celtic top of the First Division on goal average. They now needed only to win their final two League games to take the title.

Morton's next assignment was at Celtic Park on 20 April 1968. They tackled it with a footballing version of a late-1960s sit-in, their entire team planting themselves in and around their own eighteen-yard box. As the match entered its final minute, Celtic had managed to breach Morton's mob-handed defence just once but had also conceded a

breakaway goal. Then Bobby Lennox, Celtic's top scorer over the season, pounced to spin the ball into the Morton net. Celtic had been just a toe's length away from ending the season, in their terms, disastrously.

'Just before we scored,' said Stein afterwards, 'someone behind the dugout gave us the news that Rangers had won and I said to Neil Mochan, "We've lost it." Then Bobby got the goal. It couldn't have happened in a better way. I don't mean just for us, I mean for the game itself. There were 51,000 people watching and every one of them would go away happy with what they saw.'

Celtic fans were even happier the following Saturday. The club's match with Dunfermline Athletic was postponed because the Fife side were meeting Hearts in the Scottish Cup Final that day. At Ibrox, Rangers were defeated 3–2 by Aberdeen, presenting Celtic with the title. Now Celtic's visit to East End Park the following midweek would take the form of a joint celebration, with the East End Park side having triumphed in the Cup final.

The game attracted Dunfermline's official record attendance to the ground: 27,816. A further 5,000 fans were estimated to have gained illegal entry. Turnstiles were broken, roofs scaled and fifty fans were injured as the crowd were crushed together. One fan who ran on to the pitch was rugby tackled before being arrested by the police. As he was led away, Stein grabbed him by the lapels to admonish him personally, serious punishment for any Celtic fan. Celtic finished the game 2–1 victors and ended the season with sixty-three points, a record post-war total for the Scottish First Division. Over the season they had lost just one League match and had scored 106 goals, the third season in a row in which they had topped a century.

Winning the League title always had wider significance for Stein, providing, as it did, automatic entry to the European Cup. 'We are pleased about that,' said Stein. 'It's the big one, after all. I think it is a good thing for any club and any manager to be in a European tournament. But the European Cup is the tournament where you can find the European champions, where you can play Real Madrid and Benfica and other legendary teams. It is the tournament.'

A Celtic squad teeming with talent poses for the camera in August 1968, with the Glasgow Cup, the League Championship trophy and the Scottish League Cup. Back row, from left: Brogan, McGrain, McBride, Cattanach, Connelly, Fallon, Simpson, Gallagher, Quinn, Clark, Dalglish, O'Neill. Middle row: Wraith, Hughes, Hay, Craig, Jacky Clarke, Gemmell, McKellar, Murdoch, Murray, Chalmers, Livingstone. Front row: McMahon, Johnstone, Macari, Wallace, Davidson, McNeill, Wilson, Lennox, Jim Clarke, Auld, Gorman.

Since its early years, the format of the European Cup had remained intact. Every club in Europe who were champions of their country won entry to the competition. All clubs, large, middle-sized or small, then went into a draw for the opening round. Two rounds would be played before Christmas, then two more and the final in the spring. The home-and-away format militated against shock results but it did allow football supporters in the smaller nations to see the great European clubs on their doorstep. This egalitarian format had also, of course, allowed Celtic to come from nowhere and topple the great Inter Milan in 1967.

One year after the victory in Lisbon, Celtic were preparing to face the other of Milan's two massive clubs. A power shift in the Italian city had seen AC Milan emerge as champions of Italy in 1968. Now, in North America, in spring 1968, Celtic would face them in two challenge matches. 'It's possible we could meet them in the European Cup next season,' said Stein. 'This gives us the chance to assess them. You can always go to watch teams. But playing against them you learn more – and we will be learning.'

Celtic's first meeting with Milan would be at Roosevelt Stadium, New Jersey. Beforehand, Celtic would celebrate the first anniversary of the European Cup triumph. Players and officials marked the occasion with a beach barbecue in Miami, where they had spent the previous week resting and recuperating from the effects of the season. 'We'll have no sentimental tears at our celebration,' said Stein. 'We must mark it, of course. But from now on we must improve in every way, even on our European victory. We have had a great time here in Miami but football is our business and I want to use our matches here as stepping stones to another European Cup victory.'

On 26 May 1968, a 24,000 crowd saw an enthralling match between the champions of Scotland and Italy. The excitement infused the terraces and troopers at several points had to force spectators from the pitch to the stands. Willie Wallace opened the scoring in the fourteenth minute, prompting Italian fans to burst on to the pitch carrying their national flag. Milan forward Angelillo equalized before half-time. The game ended 1–1 and did much to promote 'soccer' – the purpose of such prestigious close-season matches in North America. Six days later, in front of 30,000 in Toronto, a record crowd for a match in Canada, Celtic defeated Milan 2–0, despite having two good penalty claims turned down and a goal disallowed.

Nine months later, in February 1969, a glance back at those two friendlies engendered confidence among the Celtic players as they prepared for their European Cup quarter-final. They had reached that stage with two demanding but exhilarating wins. French champions St Etienne and Yugoslavian champions Red Star Belgrade had both fallen, after considerable struggles, to an ever-improving Celtic side. Celtic and Milan, the two outstanding teams in that year's competition, were now drawn together.

Of the AC Milan team who had played in Toronto, only five men would face Celtic. Equally, Jimmy Johnstone would be new to the Italians. The winger had developed a fear of flying on returning home from the American tour in 1966 and had been exempted from Celtic's 1968 visit to North America. A week before the Milan tie, Celtic suffered a severe blow when Ronnie Simpson dislocated his shoulder in a Scottish Cup fixture at Clyde. Such an injury would have been serious enough for a young goalkeeper. It effectively ended the career of Simpson, who was thirty-eight years old, at Celtic. He would be replaced by John Fallon for the first leg of the tie, in Milan.

Before that match, at the San Siro stadium on 19 February 1969, Celtic were billeted in Varese, a mountain town north of Milan. A covering of snow greeted them on their arrival. Down in the city, conditions would be similar on the evening of the match. Protective plastic sheets were lifted from the playing surface before kick-off. Nothing could be done, however, to counter the effects of a blizzard that hampered the players and quickly rendered invisible the pitch markings.

Despite the poor visibility caused by the conditions, Celtic's intentions were entirely clear. An unusually high concentration on the defensive aspects of the game was balanced by the attacking thrusts of wingers Jimmy Johnstone and John Hughes. At centre-forward, Bobby Lennox used his pace to tear open the heart of the Milan defence. Other Celtic players would join the attack as and when necessary but chances proved to be few and far between for either side. Celtic also had a smattering of luck on the night. The defence watched anxiously as a second-half header by Angelo Sormani rebounded off the post. It was the most serious scare as Celtic held out for a 0–0 first-leg result that Stein described as 'magnificent'.

At the Marine Hotel, Troon, the night before the return at Celtic Park, the Italians broke open the champagne. This was no premature celebration – the Milan players habitually ate rice soaked in champagne to aid their digestion. Centre-forward Sormani and pivotal midfielder Giovanni Trappatoni were both injured and missing from the Milan party. The absence of two of their most potent attackers ensured that Milan would step out at Celtic Park prepared to defend in depth. They would also be ready to shuttle swiftly into attack at the slightest glimmer of a breakdown in the Celtic defence.

With the traditional European full house of 75,000 looking on, Milan got their glimpse of goal disturbingly early. After eleven minutes of Celtic pressure, Jim Craig sent a throw-in to Billy McNeill. The centre-half struggled to control the ball as it came to him. Pierino Prati, Milan's sole attacker, reacted instantly. He loosened the ball, as a dentist would ease away a decaying tooth, from under McNeill's foot. Having prised possession from his opponent, Prati accelerated away with the sleek speed of a top-grade Italian sports car. Tommy Gemmell and Jim Craig remained in his slipstream as Prati finished with finesse, his low shot flying past John Fallon's outstretched right arm.

As the crowd hushed it was possible to imagine the sound of chains clanking around the Italian defence as its locks were bolted to keep out Celtic for the remainder of the game. Celtic gamely fought on for the next seventy-nine minutes but it remained 1–0 to Milan. The Italian side went on to win the European Cup, defeating Ajax 4–1 in the final in Madrid. The hardest games of their campaign, their players acknowledged, were those against Celtic.

'Prati hit it in at the top of his run and, after that, trying to score was like hitting your head against a brick wall,' says Tommy Gemmell. 'That was a disaster because we had

Saint Etienne goalkeeper Carnus stretches to save from Billy McNeill during the second leg of the European Cup tie between the French champions and Celtic at Celtic Park in October 1968. Although Celtic were denied a goal in this instance, they would go on to a 4-0 victory against these highly skilled opponents. Jimmy Johnstone, without an equal in his ability to pull a defence out of position, was the chief inspiration behind yet another great European victory for Celtic.

Celtic players pound the turf in Varese, Italy, the day before the first leg of their European Cup quarter-final with Milan in February 1969. From left: Jim Brogan, Jimmy Johnstone, David Hay, John Hughes, Bobby Lennox, Billy McNeill (partially obscured), Jim Craig, John Clark, trainer Neil Mochan, George Connelly and Bertie Auld.

played so well in Milan. Apart from that mistake they never made any chances. We controlled the game but couldn't put the ball in the pokey hat. But you've got to take into account who you are playing against and they were a right good side.'

As was normal during the Stein years, there was too much of a buzz around Celtic Park for players or management to indulge in maudlin self-pity. As the 1968-9 season moved towards a climax, Celtic were in a position to tie up Scotland's three major trophies inside three weeks. The League Cup Final, usually an autumn fixture, had been postponed to spring because of a fire in the stand at Hampden. On 5 April 1969, Celtic finally faced Hibernian. The Celts secured their fourth successive League Cup in consummate style. A torrent of passing and movement swept Hibs away and Celtic emerged with a 6–2 win. Every Celtic goal had been a cameo of footballing class.

Three Saturdays later, at the same venue, 134,000 Old Firm fans attended the Scottish Cup Final. Each club was seeking to win the trophy for the twentieth time. Jimmy Johnstone was suspended for the final while John Hughes, Celtic's other winger, was injured. George Connelly, a new midfield talent, was picked to wear the number seven shirt in place of Johnstone. Three years previously, at the age of sixteen, Connelly had entertained the Celtic supporters before the Cup-Winners' Cup tie with Dynamo Kiev in January 1966. That evening he had accomplished several hundred keepie-uppies. He had been gradually introduced to the Celtic team over the 1968-9 season and now had the chance to show his mettle in the demanding arena of a Cup final.

After only two minutes, Bobby Lennox curled a cute corner into the heart of the Rangers penalty area. Billy McNeill rose as if on helium-pumped heels to nod the ball into an unguarded corner of the Rangers net. Rangers responded to Celtic's stylish football by battering into bruising challenges. Celtic, standing up for themselves, responded in kind. Once they had established that they would not be knocked out of their stride, there could only be one outcome.

One minute before half-time, Rangers' Orjan Persson sent a pass in the direction of Mathieson. George Connelly slid in to win the ball and push it onwards to Lennox. His thirty-yard run was capped by a sharp shot into the corner of the Rangers goal. As Rangers looked longingly towards the interval, Connelly robbed Greig of the ball on the edge of the Rangers penalty area. The youngster sent goalkeeper Martin the wrong way before rolling a left-footed shot into the net to give Celtic a 3–0 half-time lead.

With fifteen minutes remaining, Stevie Chalmers glided effortlessly down the left wing, then shaped to hit the ball to his right. His sleight of foot deceived Martin, and Chalmers quickly clipped the ball between the goalkeeper and his near post to score the final goal of the day and give Celtic a 4–0 win and the Cup. Celtic were equally superior in the League. Four days after the Scottish Cup final, they finished their League fixtures with a win at Dundee. Once again, Celtic topped the table, ending the season five points clear of Rangers. Celtic's dominance domestically could not have been more emphatic.

Billy McNeill, scorer of yet another vital Celtic goal in that Cup Final, comments: 'I've seen so many people, in the main people who probably didn't know the man as well as they might have done, saying that to big Jock the Rangers game was no more important than any other game. That is absolute nonsense. It was the most important game in the calendar for big Jock. I think it was down to the fact that that gave him the opportunity to show the Celtic support that he could beat Rangers. Nothing delighted him more than doing so. He may well have said differently publicly – but he didn't mean it, I can assure you. There was no doubt in Jock's mind which game was the most important one.'

Stein had remained loyal to the players he had inherited on his arrival at the club in 1965. They, in turn, had served him well. Yet the 1970s were around the corner and the players who had graced the 1960s could not be expected to go on forever. The successful blooding of Connelly showed that, in future, other youngsters might be smoothed into the Celtic side with minimal disruption to what had become one of the smoothest-running machines in European football. With another European Cup campaign on the horizon, however, Stein was as yet unlikely to make many dramatic changes.

Jock Stein takes the biscuit as Celtic players and their management team pose for a picture after their 1969 Scottish Cup victory. With typical thoughtfulness, Stein allows Jimmy McGrory, Stein's predecessor as manager, to take centre stage. Standing, from left: Murdoch, Simpson, Bob Rooney, Craig, Jock Stein, Chalmers, Brogan, Callaghan, Hughes. Seated: Sean Fallon, McNeill, Connelly, Lennox, Jimmy McGrory, Jimmy Steele, Gallagher, Auld, Gemmell (behind Auld), Wallace, Clark (behind Wallace), Neil Mochan, Hood. John Fallon is seated on ground.

# CHAPTER SIX
# POWER AND GLORY

Celtic's snaffling of the Scottish Cup, League Cup and League title in the space of twenty-five days in April 1969 emphasized their superiority in Scotland. Stein never underestimated the value of winning Scotland's domestic trophies but he relished the variety of challenge available in Europe even more. For Celtic, the 1969-70 European Cup began with a 2–0 aggregate dismissal of Basle of Switzerland, who had proved difficult opponents. Harry Hood, a twenty-four year old forward who had been signed by Stein for £40,000 from Clyde in the wake of the Milan defeat, had opened the scoring in the second leg at Celtic Park. Tommy Gemmell got the essential second. Along with Hood, another new face in the Celtic side for those ties was David Hay, a twenty-one year old who was fielded against Basle at right-back. Hay was a tough tackler who was also adept at forcing the ball forward constructively once he had won it.

Before the second round of the European Cup, Celtic faced St Johnstone in the League Cup Final. During the previous midweek, the Scottish national team had lost 3–2 to West Germany in Hamburg in a World Cup qualification match. Two minutes from the end of the match, Tommy Gemmell had chased German forward Helmut Haller round the pitch before landing a kick on him, an action that resulted in the Scottish player's dismissal.

At Hampden, where Celtic met St Johnstone, players had individual lockers. Gemmell, after chatting to friends outside, walked into the Celtic dressing room to find David Hay using the locker for the player who was Number Three in the Celtic team. A furious Gemmell was then peremptorily informed by Stein that he was being disciplined for his international dismissal and that David Hay was replacing him at left-back. Gemmell retorted that Stein would not have been so severe in his disciplinary measures if it had been Rangers rather than St Johnstone that Celtic had been facing in that final. A second-minute goal by Bertie Auld duly gave Celtic their fifth successive League Cup.

The following day, at a meeting with Robert Kelly and Jock Stein, Gemmell put in a transfer request. The other scorer from Lisbon in 1967, Stevie Chalmers, would also be missing from the Celtic side for a considerable period of time, having suffered a hairline fracture to his ankle against St Johnstone. Chalmers, now thirty-two years old, had been approaching the end of his Celtic career. Following this injury he would play only play half-a-dozen more times for Celtic before being transferred to Morton in 1971. Ronnie Simpson, however, would be the first Lisbon Lion to retire, a recurrence of his shoulder injury forcing him to quit the game in 1970.

Gemmell's outburst against Stein was a symptom of underlying tensions at Celtic Park. On Scotland trips, Celtic players were discovering that their pay was far below that of fellow Scots at English clubs. Some Celtic players, now used to success, were starting to question whether they were receiving their due reward for helping Celtic to prominence in Europe.

There was no freedom of contract in the 1960s, a factor that helped Stein enormously. He used that as a power and, at times, as a threat. In the 1960s the balance of power lay with the club. When a player's contract ran out, the club could write him a letter offering the minimum terms acceptable to the Scottish Football League. If the player did not agree with that, he did not get paid at all and sat in the stand. The player could not move to another club without the permission of the club that held his registration. It was a tremendous weapon and Stein used it. Players also felt aggrieved that when it came to money and contracts the manager would give the impression that the money was coming out of his and

Celtic players make their way from dressing room to pitch at East End Park, Dunfermline, for their third League fixture of the 1969-70 season. John Clark is followed by Bobby Lennox, Jimmy Johnstone, Willie Wallace, Harry Hood, Stevie Chalmers and Jim Craig. This would be the final season in which Lisbon Lions Clark and Chalmers would play significant roles in Stein's first-team plans. Ronnie Simpson, however, was the first of the Lions to give up his place at Celtic Park. He played his final ninety minutes for the first team on 11 October 1969, his 39th birthday. Two days later, in his final match for the club, he had to leave the pitch after aggravating an old shoulder injury, which caused him to announce his retirement later that season.

not Celtic's pocket. They began to wonder if he was doing enough in terms of requesting more money for his men from the board of directors.

Players, particularly front players, were terrified of getting injured. Once they were out of the team they might never win their place back. Stein would, on occasion, say that he was going to 'freshen up the team', a phrase that struck terror into the heart of any forward listening. His back four, an area requiring reliability and solidity, was kept predictable. His forward line, where quickfire responses and unpredictability were essential, were kept on their toes as to whether they would be in the team or not. Stein would frequently change players' positions or leave them out to try a variation in attack.

Bobby Murdoch was named Scottish Player of the Year in 1969. The midfield string-puller of Britain's best team was regarded by Jock Stein as Britain's best footballer. Often overshadowed by team-mates whose talents were more eye-catching, Murdoch's exceptional passing skills made him the aficionado's player.

He also knew that the bulk of the players were dyed-in-the wool Celtic supporters who had a real love of playing for the club. Again, he would use that to exert a hold on them that would not have existed had they been at any other club. This loyalty, however, only stretched in one direction – from the players to the club and not vice versa.

Tommy Gemmell was absent from Celtic's next two League games but with a second-round European Cup tie against Benfica in the offing, he and Stein made an uneasy peace. On 8 November 1969, the Saturday before the first leg with the Portuguese, Gemmell was restored to the left-back position for a League fixture with Hearts. Hay dropped out of the team but the new face of Celtic continued to be carefully sculpted. Two of Hay's reserve team-mates, inside-forwards Lou Macari, twenty years old, and Kenny Dalglish, eighteen, were in the side.

Dalglish's intricate passing in only his second League match was an encouraging sight for Celtic supporters. He and Bobby Murdoch, the 1969 Scottish Footballer of the Year, quickly tuned into each other's style of play. It wasn't enough to save Celtic from a 2–0 defeat and an overall performance that left much to be desired. It was a less than promising build-up for the first leg against Benfica. Stein, however, had rested some worldly-wise players for the Benfica game – he could afford a League defeat at that early stage of the season. For the European tie, Dalglish, Hay and Macari would look on and learn from the stand as Bertie Auld and Willie Wallace returned to the Celtic side. They had the know-how to match the Portuguese team's experienced international players, most notably Eusebio, who had been top scorer at the 1966 World Cup.

After a minute, Benfica attempted to disrupt Celtic's rhythm by conceding a free-kick in what appeared to be a harmless position. Bertie Auld trundled the ball into Tommy Gemmell's path. From twenty-five yards the full-back took out all the frustrations of the previous weeks. His hefty lunge and connection with the ball sent it soaring high into the Benfica net. Two minutes from half-time, Willie Wallace raced into the penalty area, steadied himself and, from an acute angle, nicked the ball past goalkeeper Henrique.

Eusebio, Benfica's centre-forward, and Diamentino, their outside-left, were both kept inside at half-time as Benfica coach Otto Gloria looked to stem Celtic's flow by bringing on two defenders. It worked – but only up to a point. With twenty minutes remaining, Murdoch teased the ball into the air and Harry Hood headed the ball high into the net to give Celtic a 3–0 win. The return should have been a formality but in Lisbon Celtic struggled as badly as Benfica had done in Glasgow.

Despite Stein putting out a team designed for caution, Celtic lost 3–0, with the final Benfica goal coming in the ninetieth minute. Extra-time was scoreless. Under the rules of that year's competition, the tie would now be decided by the toss of a coin. Deep inside the Stadium of

Light, the coin spun in Celtic's favour. They were in the quarter-finals but the means of getting there felt unsatisfactory, particularly to Robert Kelly, the Celtic chairman.

'Eusebio carried an injury,' says Tommy Gemmell. 'He had a great big bit of strapping on his thigh and scored a great goal but he was substituted after about an hour. We should never have lost that 3–0 lead – we were very careless at the back and gave away silly goals. The luck was with us in winning the toss of the coin but that ain't the way to win a European Cup tie.'

Together with their pride in playing for the club, a lengthy run in European football would prove a lucrative means of earning money for the Celtic players. Win bonuses boosted basic wages enormously. In this respect the Celtic players were privileged during Stein's time at the club, as no other British club's players had so many opportunities to pick up bonus money for winning in Europe.

'On a European night, there were fourteen bonuses up for grabs,' says Jim Craig. 'Everybody who played got a bonus. Those who sat on the bench shared what was left. And the figures were always the same: £125 for the first round; £250 for the second round; £500 for the quarter-finals; £750 for the semi-finals; £1500 for the final. That never changed in all the years I was at Celtic Park. Nobody mentioned inflation back then! We never had any discussions on bonuses; nobody wanted to miss out.'

Celtic had little luck with the draw for the quarter-finals of the European Cup. For the third time in four seasons they would face the champions of Italy. In the spring of 1970 that meant Fiorentina. Stein visited Florence three days before the first leg, set for Celtic Park on 4 March 1970. In the Stadio Communale he saw Celtic's next opponents slip to fourth place in the Italian League after losing to Torino. The following day he flew back to Scotland as a guest on the Italians' charter flight.

'Before a European tie, he'd have gone to see the opposition, every time, or sent somebody whom he trusted,' says Jim Craig. 'And then the [tactics] board would go up on the Tuesday night at Seamill and he would discuss how he thought they would play. He would very often say – and it's a tribute to him that we believed it – "I don't think they'll play the way I saw them. I think they'll do this on the night and they'll want us to do this." The thing about that is you've got to decide whether he was right or whether it was because we believed him that we forced them to play the way he wanted them to play. By us carrying out a counter-plan did we force them into playing a certain way? We'll never know the answer to that but he was right far more often than he was wrong.'

From the start against Fiorentina, Celtic whirred smoothly into action. From the first to the ninetieth minute they outclassed the technically accomplished Italians with a flawless display of stylish passing and movement. On the half-hour, the ball dropped to Bertie Auld on the edge of the Fiorentina penalty area. Auld, Celtic's Beau Brummel off the field, took his time to measure up the angles before sending a neatly tailored shot past Superchi in the Fiorentina goal.

Celtic's second strike of the evening had less of a dapper finish but Auld was again the man who unstitched the Italians' defence. His pacy ball into the penalty area befuddled centre-back Carpenetti, who had been brought into the Fiorentina side to solidify

Bobby Lennox raises his arm in triumph as Celtic's second goal against Italian champions Fiorentina, an own goal by the Italian side's centre-back Carpenetti, flies past goalkeeper Superchi. Italian sides rarely ran up massive goal tallies in European competition so Celtic's 3-0 first leg win in this 1970 European Cup quarter-final gave them a powerful base to build on in the return in Florence.

the defence. The defender sliced the ball high over Superchi's head to give Celtic a 2–0 lead. Auld continued to seek a way of embroidering the result with a final flourish. With masterly timing, he waited until the final minute before laying a cross on Hood's head. The striker sent the ball arcing over Superchi and towards goal. Wallace, closing in, got the final nod on the ball to give Celtic a handsome 3–0 lead to take to Italy. The result flattered the Italians. Their attempt at all-out defence had failed miserably on the night.

Fiorentina were pilloried in the Italian press for posting so many players on defensive duty at Celtic Park. They needed to put on a good show in Florence to pacify their supporters. Stein would give them little assistance. As always, he would hand his team sheet to the referee only at the last possible minute. That would leave Fiorentina manager Bruno Pesaola attempting to read the mind of the inscrutable Stein.

'The word professionalism is ill-used,' said the Celtic manager, 'but my players know exactly what it means. We must not be too clever – we must only be clever. The onus is on Fiorentina. We have lost games against Benfica and AC Milan because of carelessness and this must be avoided. We are here to confirm our place in the semi-finals.'

Resolve would be required to get the result and Stein duly switched from 4–2–4 to 4–4–2 to cramp the Italians' style. George Connelly was brought into midfield at the expense of winger John Hughes. Celtic's other wide player, Jimmy Johnstone, dropped deep throughout the match. Wallace and Lennox, Celtic's two forwards, provided Fiorentina with the constant threat of a quick breakaway. Celtic wobbled only briefly; in the ten minutes before half-time after Chiarugi had put Fiorentina 1–0 ahead. They then settled down, forced Fiorentina to play the ball sideways or backwards, and settled for a 1–0 defeat and a place in the semi-finals.

'Jock never forgot it was a battle,' says Jim Craig, 'that it was a contest as well as a game of football. He would go into a lot of pre-match detail about the opposition, but just before going out he would sometimes say to you, "By the way, I don't think this guy's too brave so let's see with your first tackle how brave he is." You must always use everything. In a European tie first time round you haven't played against your opponent before. So from the very beginning you've got to find out his strengths and weaknesses quickly.'

The last four of the 1969-70 European Cup comprised Celtic, Legia Warsaw of Poland, Feyenoord of Holland and Leeds United, the English champions. The final that the majority of football followers in Europe wished to see was an all-British decider. Instead, Celtic and Leeds were drawn together in the semis. The Leeds manager Don Revie had, in 1965, said that Scottish football would be dead in five years. Now Celtic had the chance to provide him with proof of whether or not his prognosis had been correct.

Celtic supporters outside their club's ground in March 1970, queuing for tickets for the European Cup semifinal second leg with Leeds United. The long, slow wait would prove worthwhile for those who obtained the most in-demand tickets in the history of the European Cup tournament. The tie with Leeds at Hampden Park lived up entirely to its billing.

Among the English footballing public, there was great admiration for Celtic's achievements under Stein. The majority of fans south of the border had rejoiced in a great British victory when the Celts had won in Lisbon in 1967. Key Leeds players, such as Eddie Gray, Peter Lorimer and Billy Bremner were Scots and were fully aware of Celtic's potency. In some English newspapers, however, there was a considerable degree of arrogance on behalf of Revie's Leeds. Stein was happy to use the complacent superiority exuded by the more fanciful members of the English media to fire up his players.

In England, the Scottish League was regarded as being deeply inferior to the English one. The English usually conveniently forgot that their League had been founded in 1888 by a Scot, the visionary William McGregor of Aston Villa. The English First Division was, indeed, more intensively competitive than its Scottish equivalent. Stein and his players, however, judged themselves by their own high standards and not by whether they proved superior to their opponents in Scotland. Those standards had been raised to considerable heights through Celtic's stirring jousts with the best clubs in Europe.

'We won't play as we did against Fiorentina in Italy. We were holding a 3–0 lead then but in this tie we have nothing to defend.'

The Celtic players had a collective and individual pride that meant they hated to get beaten. Even training was very competitive under Stein. He would get two players to pick sides – one with bibs and one without. He would then watch how the games went. If they were competitive he would leave those sides to play each other for days or weeks at a time. He always wanted competition in training and he got it because there was fierce rivalry for first-team places. Stein understood deeply his team's personalities and their attitudes. He would then play them all off against each other. On one trip to America, running tensions resulted in the players having a monumental scrap among themselves. That suited Jock Stein because it meant his team was on edge. It pleased him that his players were, mentally, fighting fit.

Four days before the first leg with Leeds, a 0–0 draw with Hearts at Tynecastle gave Celtic their fifth consecutive First Division title. They would finish the season twelve points clear of Rangers, the most commanding winning margin during Stein's years at Celtic. On the same Saturday, Leeds kept six key players sidelined for their match with Southampton: Billy Bremner, Johnny Giles, Mick Jones, Paul Reaney, Norman Hunter and Terry Cooper. Two days before the Celtic match, Leeds fielded a reserve outfit against Derby County. It led to the English champions losing both games and, almost certainly, that year's English League title. It was obvious where their priorities lay.

Approximately 10,000 Celtic fans would be in the 45,000 crowd at Elland Road, Leeds, for the first leg of the European Cup semi-final on 1 April 1970. 'One thing is certain,' said Stein. 'We won't play as we did against Fiorentina in Italy. We were holding a 3–0 lead then but in this tie we have nothing to defend.' Leeds were back to full strength for the visit of Celtic but, as in the encounters with Benfica and Fiorentina, the tone of the tie was set from the first minute. George Connelly's shot from the edge of the penalty area took the most minute of deflections and went skimming past Gary Sprake in the Leeds United goal. Connelly scored a better goal in the second half but it was inexplicably disallowed. It ended 1–0 to Celtic, a great result but one that failed to do justice to Celtic's mesmeric control of the game that spring evening. From first to last they had dominated the match, surging into attack after attack with seemingly effortless élan.

None of the Leeds players could get a handle on Jimmy Johnstone even though at various times half their team seemed to be trying to pin him down. The Leeds players had achieved success through Revie's high-grade, systematic style but they could not cope with Celtic's craftsmanship and invention. Such creativity, allied to work rate, was something Leeds did not face in the English League. On the day after the match, the Celtic players returned to Glasgow by train, arriving at Central Station. There, the 'Celtic Song' bounced off the walls as 5,000 supporters greeted their heroes.

On the Saturday before the return with Leeds, Celtic had the opportunity to tie up their third Scottish trophy of the season. On 11 April they were at Hampden Park for the Scottish Cup Final against Aberdeen. Unlike Revie, there was no possibility of Stein 'resting' a large chunk of his team. 'The Scottish Cup is not going to be sacrificed because we play Leeds United on Wednesday,' he said. 'Our fans will not allow us to take it easy in any match.'

It would prove a disturbing afternoon for Celtic. Referee Bobby Davidson awarded a soft penalty to Aberdeen in the twenty-seventh minute, ruling that the ball had struck a Celtic arm. The Celtic player concerned, Bobby Murdoch, maintained afterwards that the ball had come off his chest. As Celtic pursued an equalizer, Bobby Clark, the Aberdeen goalkeeper, dropped the ball at Lennox's feet. The forward popped it into the net. The referee, however, had spotted an infringement missed by the other 108,000 present and disallowed the goal. Another grim Davidson decision followed when Lennox was denied a penalty after a challenge from Dons captain Martin Buchan had sent him tumbling to the turf.

Buoyed by these decisions in their favour, Aberdeen scored twice in the final ten minutes before Lennox got Celtic's only reply in the last seconds of the match. Stein, who normally kept his own counsel on matters of controversy, complained vociferously about the refereeing afterwards. The 3–1 defeat had ended his hopes of a third treble in four years.

As the 1969-70 season drew to a close, Celtic were in the process of spending £100,000 on concreting and improving the east terracing at Celtic Park. The gradient of the steps was being increased to make viewing easier for fans. With that section of Celtic Park out of action, the return leg with Leeds, on 15 April 1970, would be played at Hampden Park to accommodate the expected crowd. The previous European Cup record attendance had been set at Hampden on 18 May 1960 for the final between Real Madrid and Eintracht Frankfurt. All 134,000 tickets had been sold for that game but a crowd of 127,621 had turned up on the night; more than 6,000 individuals had failed to take their places on the terraces.

In anticipation of their place in the European Cup semi-finals, Celtic had begun printing tickets a week before their second leg with Fiorentina. Prices ranged from ten shillings to £1 for the terracing and from £1 to £2 10s (£2.50) for the stand. On Sunday 22 March 1970, three-and-a-half weeks before the home tie with Leeds, tickets went on sale to the public at Celtic Park. The queues stretched from the stand down through the main car park and out on to London Road. Buyers paid for their ticket at a turnstile, then went into the ground, walked across the west terracing and exited into Janefield Street. Within two hours, all 60,000 available tickets had been sold. The remaining 75,000 tickets would go to Celtic supporters' clubs and to Leeds United fans.

The controversial manner of their Cup Final defeat meant that the Celtic players remained dispirited as they assembled at Seamill the next day to prepare for the match with Leeds. Gradually, their spirits lifted as Stein primed them carefully for the European Cup tie. Half an hour before kick-off, the Celtic players received a massive boost when Billy McNeill was passed fit to play. He had received a nasty ankle injury in the match with Aberdeen.

Celtic would, however, be without Willie Wallace, which meant Stein moving John Hughes from the wing to centre-forward. In March 1965, shortly after Stein had taken over as manager of Celtic, Hughes had scored twice with headers for the Scottish League against the English League at Hampden Park. His direct opponent had been Leeds' centre-half Jack Charlton, who had ended that evening thoroughly disorientated. Now the two men would face each other again.

After fourteen minutes, a typical piece of Scottish invention saw a twenty-five-yard shot twist and turn into the roof of a Hampden net. Billy Bremner stood to receive deserved acclaim from his Leeds team-mates as the 136,505 at Hampden were temporarily silenced. The goal served only to provide the overture for a Celtic performance suitable to set in front of the record crowd to witness a European Cup match anywhere on the continent.

Twice before half-time Leeds players cleared off their own line as Celtic pounded incessantly at their goal. McNeill, fighting the pain from his ankle, forgot his own troubles to urge his men on. Jimmy Johnstone went bobbing, weaving, ducking and darting amidst the English team's defenders. They looked ponderous and musclebound in their efforts to cope with his mercurial moves. Connelly, Auld and Murdoch gave the Leeds midfielders a lesson in the arts of the game of football. Lennox, with his pace, and Hughes, with his power, had the Leeds defence performing contortions in their efforts to combat the Celtic men.

With forty-seven minutes gone, Bertie Auld caressed a cross into the heart of the Leeds penalty area. John Hughes inched in front of Jack Charlton to nick an elegant diving header past Sprake. Five minutes later, Murdoch poked a pass to Johnstone on the right flank. Some typical trickery from the Celtic winger drew Terry Cooper and Norman Hunter to him. That created space for Murdoch on the edge of the Leeds penalty area. When Johnstone rolled the ball into his path the way was clear for the midfielder to shoot low and hard past substitute goalkeeper David Harvey.

The biggest surprise of the evening was that the scoring ended at 2–1 to Celtic although Hughes, in the final minute, had a shot cleared off the Leeds goal-line. Even 3–1 would not have done justice to Celtic's superiority – only an extravagant scoreline would have provided the necessary emphasis. For those present, it was enough that they had seen Leeds thoroughly beaten on the evening. For twenty minutes after the final whistle the fans stayed and bayed for the players to receive public acclaim for their performance. Eventually, the Celtic players surfaced from the depths of the stadium for the first post-match lap of honour at Hampden since the League Cup Final five years previously.

'Wee Jinky was out of this world at Elland Road!' says Tommy Gemmell. 'Terry Cooper, the Leeds left-back, must have nightmares every time somebody mentions Jimmy Johnstone because he gave him a total going over. Norman Hunter was shouting to Cooper, "Kick him!" Cooper said, "You come out and kick him." Hunter came out and tried to stick it on wee Jimmy. Wee Jimmy just waltzed round about him, nutmegged him and everything.

'We all played well. In fact, those were two of the easiest ties I experienced in Europe. I was playing against Peter Lorimer and he made it so easy for me to mark him it was unbelievable. I got the impression that he was there for free-kicks and corner-kicks. He never at any time tried to take me on. He would just knock it inside to Bremner or someone else. It was the same at Hampden in the second game. Leeds went away with their tails between their legs and, of course, that put all the English media's gas at a peep.

'The English-based media were a bit peeved because they had built them up like nobody's business. This team, Revie's machine, were

A rare sight on the night of the second leg of the European Cup semi-final between Celtic and Leeds United: Terry Cooper, the Leeds left-back, winning the ball from Jimmy Johnstone. The winger's trickery was too much for Cooper to cope with and Johnstone's wing work was essential in prising open the Leeds defence in both legs of the tie. Leeds had won the English First Division with a record points total the previous season. The challenge of defeating such a strong side, combined with the extra spice provided by a Scottish-English confrontation, brought out the very best in the Celtic players.

Teeming terraces at Hampden provide a suitably spectacular backdrop as Bobby Murdoch's shot speeds towards the Leeds net. Watching over it are, from left: George Connelly, John Hughes and Bobby Lennox of Celtic. Goalkeeper David Harvey and Paul Madeley are the defeated Leeds players.

supposed to be invincible. Every one of them was an internationalist and we gave them a going over twice. I don't think we actually realized how good we were. I think we sometimes underestimated ourselves. It suited us that the English media were brainwashing their own people because everyone was expecting us to take a fall. And then, of course, we were saying to ourselves, "We're playing an English side, aren't we?"

'The English papers afterwards made excuses for Leeds, saying they had been exhausted by playing too many games in too many competitions. We played more games than Leeds that season! Of course, the English media think that because they play in the English League that the games are harder than in the Scottish League. You've still got to go out there and work your socks off for ninety minutes – it doesn't matter which League you're playing in. If you went out there and went through the motions big Jock wouldn't have you in the side. You would just be ditched. It was as simple as that. If you weren't pulling your weight you were out.'

Celtic's opponents in the European Cup Final in Milan on 6 May 1970 were Feyenoord of Rotterdam. They had defeated Legia Warsaw 2–0 on aggregate in the less high-profile semi-final. They had also knocked out the holders, AC Milan, in the second round. In late April Stein travelled to Holland to watch Feyenoord draw 3–3 with Ajax. It was unusual for Feyenoord to concede so may goals in a match: over the entire League season prior to that game they had conceded just eleven. They now had problems in goal where Eddie Treytel was suffering a severe loss of form.

Celtic, meanwhile, would travel to Milan via Fraserburgh. With the Scottish League season having ended on 18 April, Stein arranged a friendly with the Highland League side on 27 April, which Celtic won 7–0. Then, on the evening of Friday 1 May, at Celtic Park, 6,000 looked on as Celtic worked their way gently through an 8–0 friendly win over Second Division sparring partners Stenhousemuir.

On 3 May 1970 Stein sat down with his players to inform them of his assessment of Feyenoord's strengths and weaknesses. Celtic flew to Milan the following day. In the two days before the match they would be based at Varese, where they had prepared for their European Cup quarter-final with Milan the previous year. Celtic had been invited by AC Milan to use their sumptuous training headquarters. Stein had declined this invitation, fearing that this would alienate Italian supporters of other clubs.

Being based at Varese meant the players were well away

from the attentions of their supporters. In Lisbon in 1967, Stein had felt that supporters' easy access to the team's hotel had caused a distraction. He had been so worried by the constant demands of the fans then that he had taken his players away from the hotel the night before the match to watch an international friendly live on TV at the house of an acquaintance who lived in Portugal. Ernst Happel, the Feyenoord manager, based his squad at Cernobbio for similar reasons. In common with Varese, the Dutch side's headquarters was approximately thirty miles from Milan.

'Feyenoord are more or less in the same position as we were in 1967,' said Stein on arrival in Italy that Monday. 'We were the underdogs then, with nothing to lose. If we had not won, no one would have worried too much. While we are confident of winning I cannot agree with the current impression that Celtic cannot be beaten. As far as I am concerned it is certainly a problem and an attitude I don't fancy at all. Mind you, the occasion should bring out the best in our team. They won't be professionals if they are caught out by all this talk at this stage and I will be driving the point home to them in our discussions after training tomorrow.'

Celtic fans had received 15,000 European Cup Final tickets, at £1 and £2, which were distributed by the Scottish Football Association. Another 5,000 Celtic supporters, some based on the continent, obtained tickets from the Italian FA. The Celtic fans arrived in a Milan strangulated by industrial action. There were even fears that the final might not be played at the appointed time due to the threat of action from electricians responsible for the floodlighting. However, those fears soon receded and the Italian FA offered assurances that the game would go ahead.

'The English papers afterwards made excuses for Leeds, saying they had been exhausted by playing too many games in too many competitions. We played more games than Leeds that season!'

Stein anticipated Feyenoord adopting an Italian-style defensive game in the final. He believed the Dutch team's players did not have the pace of his own men. The Celtic manager anticipated that if Celtic attacked them with gusto, Feyenoord would be overwhelmed in much the same way as Inter's game had been disrupted three years previously. This led to him adopting an adventurous 4–2–4 formation for the Final. With Johnstone and Hughes on the wings and Wallace and Lennox through the middle, Celtic had pace in each of the four forward positions. Auld and Murdoch would be asked to control affairs in the middle of the park. 'We must attack the game,' said Stein, 'and stretch the Dutch defence from the start. Our wingers may present Feyenoord with a situation they have never encountered in their previous rounds. No one knows exactly how they will react to our attacking style.'

Feyenoord lined up in a 4–3–3 formation. Their midfield comprised Dutch internationals Wim van Hanegem and Wim Jansen and the Austrian Franz Hasil. Those three began as they meant to continue, shuttling the ball around the midfield with exceptional assurance. Murdoch and Auld, who was now thirty-two years old, had too much legwork to do against the Dutch side's midfield trio. Overwhelmed in that area of the field, Celtic found the game slipping away from them. In addition, Jim Brogan, at centre-back on the night, received a first-minute injury that hampered him for the rest of the match. Stein opted not to substitute him.

Celtic had their chances early in the game. After twenty minutes Wallace's shot was half-stopped by Eddie Pieters Graafland, who was playing his first game of the season after replacing Treytel. When the ball ran loose, Lennox sharply steered it into the net. The Celtic celebrations were just beginning when Concetto Lo Bello, the Italian referee, brought his whistle to his lips to signal offside, a decision as slow as Lennox's reactions had been swift.

On the half-hour, that element of bad luck appeared to matter little. A foul on Wallace

Jock Stein congratulates his captain Billy McNeill after Celtic's victory in the epic encounter with Leeds at Hampden.

saw a free-kick awarded to Celtic twenty yards from goal. Bobby Murdoch cleverly teased a backheel into Tommy Gemmell's path. The full-back connected powerfully with the ball and it pelted low into the Feyenoord net. This time Celtic were provided with assistance by Lo Bello, who had run across Pieters Graafland's line of vision as the kick was being taken. 'The referee helped me,' says Tommy Gemmell. 'They'd left a gap in the wall, so I thought I'd just have a go. I kept it on target and hit it and the referee had to jump out of the way of it. Maybe that flummoxed the goalkeeper.' Two minutes later, as the ball pinged around the Celtic penalty area, Rinus Israel, the Feyenoord centre-back, sprang into the air to send the ball looping high over Celtic goalkeeper Evan Williams' head and into the top right-hand corner of the net.

Celtic had been struggling, in the first half hour, to get into their groove. Now the desolation of losing a goal immediately after scoring one left them reeling. They hung on until half-time but in the second half Feyenoord exerted an iron grip on the game. It was Celtic's first taste of Dutch total football, where a team would defend as one and then push forward as one. Defenders were expected to be able to exchange positions with attackers and attackers to take on the mantle of defenders as and when required. Feyenoord, under their Austrian coach Happel, were the first club in Europe to perfect this style and they played it to perfection in Milan.

The Dutch team's players flooded forward time and time again and went closest to scoring when a shot from Hasil cracked off the foot of a Celtic post. Celtic managed to reach the ninetieth minute with the score still at 1–1. The additional half-hour began with the running of Hughes creating a scoring chance. The winger, however, knocked the ball against Pieters Graafland when he should have deposited it in the back of the Dutch net.

For most of the additional thirty minutes Celtic again held out under exceptional pressure from the Dutch. With three minutes to go, a replay two days later appeared the most likely outcome. Then a high ball from midfield flew over McNeill's head. As Ove Kindvall, Feyenoord's Swedish striker, swept in behind him, McNeill, stumbling backwards, handled the ball in mid-air. The ball dropped for Kindvall to control it quickly on his chest, toe-poke it past Williams and make the score 2–1.

There is no doubt that Feyenoord, on their overall play, deserved to win. However, had Kindvall fluffed his shot and missed the target or had Williams got to the ball first, Lo Bello would almost certainly have awarded a penalty for McNeill's clear handling of the ball. It was less a matter of the referee playing the advantage than of him having had no time to stop play because the action had unfolded so quickly. Imagine the Feyenoord players' outrage had Kindvall missed and the referee had then indicated he had played the advantage rule when McNeill's handball had been seen clearly on television screens across Europe!

It was patently wrong that Lo Bello allowed the goal simply because the Dutch side had scored. It meant, in practice, that Feyenoord had two chances to get their 117th minute winner: Kindvall put the ball in the net so they got a goal but had he missed they would almost certainly have been given a penalty. The inescapable conclusion, therefore, is that Lo Bello did not apply the rules correctly in awarding Feyenoord's second goal. In effect, he appeared to have played the advantage after the event, something not within his remit.

The Celtic players and Stein, being the good sportsmen they were, accepted defeat gracefully, conceding they had lost to the superior team on the night. 'The better team won,' said Stein, dignified at the scene of defeat. 'We had too many players off form. I know the reason but I am not going to criticize my players in public. We are disappointed. I was surprised we played so badly but in saying this I don't want to take away any credit from the other side. Every one of their team was a good player.' The beaten Celtic side was:

Williams, Hay, Gemmell, Murdoch, McNeill, Brogan, Johnstone, Wallace, Hughes, Auld (Connelly), Lennox.

In the following days, rumours spread that 'the reason' referred to by Stein was his displeasure at the players' involvement in financial negotiations in setting up a player pool independent of the club. The players had planned money-raising ventures from the Final, such as a caravan outside Celtic Park selling souvenirs endorsed by them. In the wake of the Feyenoord defeat this was put on hold. '1970 was an attempt by the players to organize themselves into a commercial enterprise,' says Jim Craig. 'It was nothing to do with the bonus, it was entirely separate from the club. And it was done too late and it was done at an unfortunate time, which was just before the game.'

Jimmy Johnstone finds the going tough against Feyenoord's disciplined defence in the 1970 European Cup Final at the San Siro, Milan.

'We were unlucky in the sense that our season had basically finished whereas theirs was still going on,' says Billy McNeill. 'They were still much more battle-sharpened than we were but I think our whole preparation was far too relaxed and easy. There was too much thought given to what should happen afterwards – should we get an open-decked bus to travel through the streets of Glasgow. There was no disgrace in losing to a team as good as Feyenoord but I would like to go back and have the preparations much more realistic and to the point than they were.'

'On the night,' says Jim Craig, who was a substitute in Milan, 'Brogie didn't do us any favours because when Brogie got injured he stayed on. He should have come off but I can appreciate why he would have wanted to carry on. Brogie missed out in 1967 so in 1970 he was desperate to play on. But you could see he was not running freely and I don't know why Jock chose to keep him on. I thought at the time the logical thing to do was take him off, move Davie Hay into midfield, put me on at right-back and say, "It's not our night. Let's just sit on this and go for a draw. There's a replay on Friday." It's easy to be wise after the event but don't forget that Jock was not comfortable with substitutes. Maybe he didn't want to take a risk.'

Celtic's goalscorer, Tommy Gemmell, comments, 'Nobody ever talks to me about the goal I scored against Feyenoord. People say, "What about that goal you scored in the European Cup Final?" And my first question is, "Which Final are you talking about?" It just shows you that when you are losers nobody wants to know. When you are winners everybody wants to know. If we could have held on to our lead for fifteen or twenty minutes and consolidated we might have won it even though we weren't playing well.'

The day after the defeat, as reality bit in hard, the Celtic fans suffered massive delays in getting to the airport by public transport or found themselves paying outrageous sums for taxi journeys. Once there, they found chaos, with the Italian officials unable to cope with the influx of passengers and aircraft in the wake of the Final. The official Celtic party found their own flight seriously delayed and had to spend eight gloomy hours in a basement room of the airport. It was all so different from the effervescent atmosphere in the twenty-four hours after they had won the trophy in Lisbon. Those dark moments emphasized to Stein that radical action was required if Celtic were to emerge into football's sunlight once again.

73

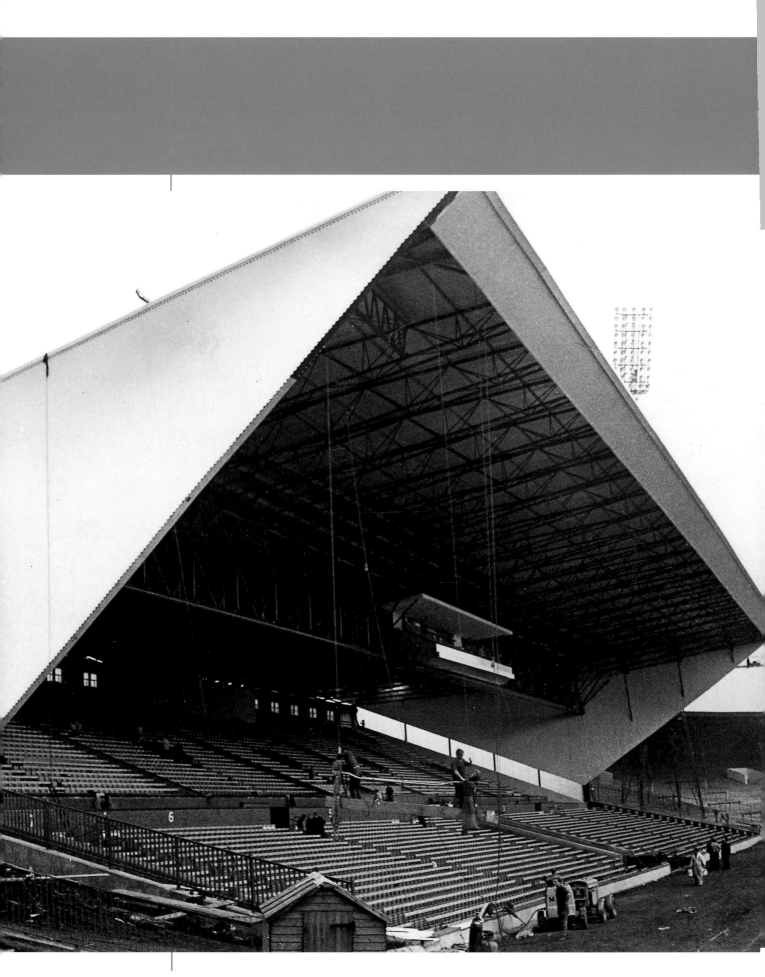

# CHAPTER SEVEN

# SEVENTIES SUCCESSES

A VISIT TO THE NEW WORLD WAS INTENDED TO HELP HERALD CELTIC'S NEW ERA IN THE WAKE OF THE 1970 European Cup Final. On 11 May, five days after the defeat by Feyenoord, a sixteen-man squad flew out for a tour of North America. Kenny Dalglish and George Connelly were in the party. Also on the trip were Lou Macari and nineteen year old Vic Davidson, another promising forward. 'It's not a disappointment that will break us,' said Stein looking back on the events in Milan. 'It might even make us. If we had won the Cup – and we wanted to win it badly – we might have mistakenly taken the attitude that the present team could have gone on forever.'

Stein, however, was too wise to do anything other than take a patient approach to the reconstruction of his side. The youngsters would be introduced over time, allowing them to find their feet at first-team level without being put under excessive pressure. The manager, however, could have been forgiven if he had pushed his youngsters into place too quickly: some of his more experienced men were testing his patience.

Six days after flying out to America, Stein returned to Scotland. Jimmy Johnstone, who was not on the trip through a combination of an ankle injury and his fear of flying, was demanding higher wages or a transfer. Johnstone, who had not long before signed a long-term contract, was told Celtic's policy was not to keep players who were unhappy with their terms. After discussions with Stein, the player made his peace with the club. On the day after Stein had flown home, Tommy Gemmell and Bertie Auld were reported to have insulted a waitress at a Celtic supporters' function in New Jersey. They were ordered to pack their bags and return to Scotland.

The 1970-1 season saw the draws for the early rounds of the European Cup being kind, for once, to Celtic. Kokkola of Finland were swept aside by a 14–0 aggregate. Waterford of Ireland, in the second round, were equally easy opponents, Celtic moving into the quarter-finals on a 10–2 aggregate. Conversely, competition in the Scottish League was proving more testing than usual. As Celtic prepared to face Aberdeen for the first time in the League that season, on 12 December 1970, the Dons were just one point behind the Glaswegians at the top of the First Division.

Such was the seriousness with which Stein was treating this game that he took his players to Seamill to prepare. A massive crowd of 63,000 was enticed along to Celtic Park to witness a clash of styles. Celtic remained a team that, whatever their formation, relied on magical moments of inspiration from their players to win a game. Aberdeen were more systematic in their approach, stolidly retaining possession until a breach in the opposition's defence revealed itself.

When, on that December afternoon, one such opening appeared in the Celtic defence after fifty-three minutes, Aberdeen striker Joe Harper stole in to steal the lead. Celtic were highly inventive in their response but couldn't equalize. They conceded defeat and the leadership of the League. Three weeks later, on 2 January 1971, Celtic dropped another League point. An eighty-ninth minute goal by Jimmy Johnstone had looked set to give Celtic a 1–0 win in the New Year Old Firm match, at Ibrox. However, one minute later Colin Stein equalized for Rangers.

The scoring details, however, were entirely overshadowed by the tragic events at the end of the match, when sixty-six people were crushed to death on Stairway 13 at Ibrox. Players and officials of both clubs, in the succeeding days, joined forces to mourn the

An ultra-modern stand takes shape at Celtic Park in the summer of 1971. Its roof is a streamlined, cantilevered construction, free of posts or pillars that might block views of the action. It covers 10,000 new, plastic seats. A futuristic press box is suspended over the heads of seated spectators. Nothing like this had been seen previously inside a football ground in Scotland. It was not, however, a total demolition of the stand that had been built in 1929; its classic external facade would be retained. Elsewhere in the ground, conditions remained basic. During the Jock Stein years, only slight modifications were made to the terraces although roofs were added to cover both ends.

dead at church services. Later that January, an Old Firm select met a Scotland eleven to raise funds for those bereaved by the Ibrox disaster – an 80,000-plus crowd attended the match held at Ibrox.

In the autumn of 1970, Celtic had, for the first time, lost a League Cup Final under Stein, going down 1–0 to Rangers. Domestically, Stein would, at best, have to settle for a League and Cup double. A 7–1 win over Raith Rovers in a Scottish Cup quarter-final on 6 March 1971 helped his team progress towards that target. Before the game, however, John Hughes, angry at being left out of the team, handed Stein a written transfer request. He was sent home by the manager.

Hughes remembers those days clearly. 'He [Stein] used to say, "I'll put you in the stand for six weeks. If he did that you lost your bonuses. I remember we played Airdrie in the semi-finals of the Cup in 1971 and we drew 3–3 with them. And afterwards I had an argument with him. So I fell out with him, he dropped me and I didn't play another game that season.

'I had a wife, two kids and a mortgage and my take-home pay at Celtic Park was £33. At Celtic they made a big thing about a squad system being in operation but it was him [Stein] who decided who was in the squad and if he dropped you you missed out on bonuses. So that's how much control he had over things – because you needed to be in the team to survive. Nowadays, if a player is earning £3,000 or £4,000 a week and the manager threatens to put them in the stand they'll go and sit there quite happily. He was very good at his job but he ruled by fear.'

Hughes was dropped from the squad that flew out to Amsterdam on Monday 8 March for Celtic's European Cup quarter-final first leg with Ajax. There was some light relief for Stein and the Celtic party the night before the game. The coach of a local women's side asked if his team could provide Celtic with opposition for a practice match. Stein politely declined, explaining that he and his players were in Holland on serious business.

The gravity of the task was apparent from kick-off in Amsterdam's Olympic Stadium the following evening as Celtic found themselves pressed into desperate defence. Ajax, inspired by the talents of the twenty-three year old Johan Cruyff, created chance after chance. Celtic rarely got near the Ajax goalmouth. After a couple of escapes in their own penalty area they managed to reach half-time with the score pegged at 0–0.

There would be no respite in the second half. Cruyff fired in a shot that was booted off the line by Brogan. Then Johan Neeskens, who only nine months previously had starred for Holland in an international youth tournament in Scotland, picked out Cruyff with a header. Sweeping swiftly on to the ball, Cruyff sent it flying past Williams for the opener.

With twenty minutes to go, Barry Hulshoff shaped to take a free-kick on the edge of the Celtic penalty area. Spotting a chink of light in the defensive wall, he steered the ball through the gap and past Evan Williams. The final minute arrived with Celtic still trailing 2–0. Then Piet Kiezer sent a wounding shot past Williams. The 3–0 defeat, allied to the style and power of Ajax's football, gave Celtic only the most slender of hopes for the second leg.

Jim Craig wins the ball from Johan Cruyff as Celtic take on Ajax in their 1971 European Cup quarter-final in Amsterdam.

On their return to Glasgow the following day, Stein took his players for an afternoon training session. Ever the optimist, he managed to retrieve some hope from the situation. 'We have an hour and a half to do to Ajax what they did to us in twenty-five minutes,' he said. He also pointed to previous great home performances against top-grade opposition, notably the 5–1 and 4–0 wins over Red Star Belgrade and St Etienne respectively in the 1968-9 European Cup.

On Ajax's arrival in Glasgow two days before the return, Cruyff was nursing a heavy cold. 'When Cruyff has a cold, all of Ajax has a cold,' said his manager Rinus Michels of the man who had already been named Dutch Player of the Year three times. But on the night the forward was fit to take his place in front of 84,000 at Hampden Park.

With close to half an hour gone, Tommy Callaghan headed the ball on to Johnstone, whose close-range shot made it 1–0 to Celtic. Gerry Muhren almost got a quick equalizer for Ajax with a shot that clattered off the foot of a post. Throughout the match, Celtic had more of the ball but they struggled to construct hard-hitting chances, although a header from McNeill forced goalkeeper Heinz Stuy into a difficult save. At the opposite end, McNeill's defensive partner Jim Brogan prevented an Ajax goal when he nicked the ball off Cruyff's toe as the Dutchman prepared to shoot. It ended 1–0 to Celtic but it was Ajax who progressed to the semi-finals and, in May 1971, to victory in the Final itself. It was the third season in succession that Celtic had lost to the eventual European Cup winners.

An opportunity for a sixth successive European Cup run would depend heavily on Celtic's return Scottish First Division fixture with Aberdeen, on 17 April 1971. The Dons had maintained their challenge for Celtic's title and an all-ticket 35,000 crowd turned up at Pittodrie to see if the north's leading lights could produce a performance to outshine Celtic's stars.

With three minutes gone, Jimmy Johnstone's corner fell to Harry Hood on the edge of the six-yard box. He flicked the ball past Aberdeen goalkeeper Bobby Clark to put Celtic 1–0 ahead. Shortly before half-time Evan Williams let slip a cross and Alex Willoughby equalized for the Dons. In the second half, Williams was rounded by Aberdeen's Arthur Graham, who pushed the ball towards the gaping goal. Billy McNeill raced back to deflect the winger's shot away from the target. The match, which had been thoroughly engaging throughout, ended 1–1. It left Celtic three points behind Aberdeen at the top of the League table. Celtic had three games left to play, Aberdeen just one.

Since the Ajax defeat, rumours had grown that Stein was on the verge of leaving Celtic to become Manchester United manager. After the Aberdeen game, he said: 'I will be staying here as long as I am needed. We have been through a lot together in the last six glorious years and you don't break these links so easily. There is still much to do.' Encouraged by this news, his players went on to score ten goals in their final three games, finishing the season two points clear of Aberdeen at

Leaping between Ruud Krol and Barry Hulshoff, Billy McNeill rises to the challenge of putting pressure on the Ajax defence during the second leg of Celtic's European Cup quarter-final with the Dutch team in the spring of 1971.

the top of the Scottish First Division. The season ended nicely with Celtic completing the double by winning the Scottish Cup. Two goals in a first-half minute, from Macari and Hood, led to a 2–1 replay victory over Rangers after the first match had ended 1–1. A total of 225,000 people had attended the two matches at Hampden.

Five months later, on 23 October 1971, Celtic would once again be at Hampden, this time for their sixth successive League Cup Final. A 63,000 crowd turned up, the smallish attendance for a final indicating that a Celtic victory was seen as something of a formality. The Celtic contingent who did attend anticipated the event like theatregoers who attend a classic play time and again. They expected to witness a predictable but still enjoyable demolition of inferior opponents. In this case, the team expected to be bit-part players was Partick Thistle. The team from the Maryhill area of Glasgow had been promoted to the First Division at the same time as Celtic had been wrapping up the 1970-1 League title.

Celtic's leading man, Billy McNeill, was missing through injury. The absence of central defensive authority was obvious as Thistle powered to a quite incredible 4–0 lead in twenty-five first-half minutes. At Thistle's fourth goal, five Celtic players stood stock still in a line as a cross was delivered from the right wing. Thistle centre-forward Jimmy Bone could even afford to miscontrol the ball as Williams stood rooted to his goal-line, allowing his opponent to steady himself before putting the ball in the net.

Kenny Dalglish pulled a goal back midway through the second half but the 4–1 defeat made Celtic Park a sombre place in the succeeding days. It signalled the end of Tommy Gemmell's career at Celtic. 'I fell out a wee bit with big Jock and got transferred to Nottingham Forest. I didn't want to leave Celtic at all and I'd have loved to have finished my career at Celtic Park. But by 1971, when I left, I think Jock and I had lost a bit of mutual respect for each other. I think when you lose that you are better not being there. If he had said to me, "Right, let's bury the hatchet and get on with things," I think I would have probably said, "Fine, let's go." '

For Celtic's next fixture, a League match at Dunfermline, goalkeeper Evan Williams was replaced by Denis Connaghan, a twenty-six year old signed from Dunfermline two days after the League Cup Final. Williams had struggled badly against Celtic's poor relations from Maryhill. Earlier that October, Willie Wallace and John Hughes had been transferred to Crystal Palace.

On the final day of October 1971, Dixie Deans, a twenty-five year old striker, was signed from Motherwell for £17,500. Throughout Stein's term, the club was never, as buyers, big players in the transfer market. As sellers, Celtic were very much in the big league. Their players, backed by solid European experience and with honours degrees in football learning under Stein, could command high fees. The sales of Gemmell, Hughes and Wallace, all of whom had passed their peaks, raked in £85,000 late in 1971.

In the boardroom, Robert Kelly, who was seriously ill throughout 1971 and who died late that year, had been replaced by Desmond White as chairman. White presided over an ongoing arrangement whereby Celtic would use only a small proportion of a considerable transfer income to buy new players. Stein's winning of the European Cup with a team that had cost next to nothing had, to some extent, worked against him – it set a precedent for the remainder of his term as manager.

In 1972, looking back on the League Cup Final, Stein said: 'I believe that we are capable of losing the next game we play. And I try to gear the players up to the fact that we are capable of losing the next game. The biggest blow we ever had as a club was the League Cup Final last year when Partick Thistle beat us 4–1. Not from the defeat but because before the game lots of our players thought defeat was impossible.

'That was a sign to us that things had to change. We needed players who were hungry again. We needed to get going again. We needed to believe that people could beat us. We needed to believe that once we stepped over the white line to start the game that we had to make things happen for us. In that match, we just thought it was a matter of going out and things would automatically happen for us. Once that was out of the way it was near the end of the season before we lost a match again.'

At the time of the 1971 League Cup Final, Aberdeen had again been leading Celtic in the League. The Celts, however, would lose only one League game between then and the end of the season, finishing ten points clear of the Pittodrie club and sixteen ahead of Rangers. These were exceptional margins in an era when two points remained the prize for a League win. Stein's warnings to avoid complacency had been well received by the players.

The substantial lead meant that by the time Celtic approached the first leg of their third European Cup semi-final, on 5 April 1972, Stein could concentrate all his resources on his favourite competition. Victories over BK 1903 Copenhagen, Sliema Wanderers and Ujpest Dozsa, the champions of Denmark, Malta and Hungary respectively, had taken Celtic to the rarefied heights of a second European Cup meeting with Internazionale Milan. The first leg took place at the San Siro, where Inter were unbeaten in eighteen European Cup ties.

The Italians feared committing themselves to all-out attack in case Celtic obtained a vital away goal while Celtic were confident of their chances of making an attacking game of it at Celtic Park. Consequently, Stein adopted a 4–5–1 formation with Scots-Italian Lou Macari as the sole attacker. With caution the order of the day, neither side created many chances and the game petered out into a 0-0 draw. Celtic's performance was particularly notable as several of their players were in their first full season as members of the first team. Macari and Dalglish showed commendable composure while nineteen year old defender Pat McCluskey, who had made only two previous appearances for the club, both as substitute, successfully replaced Jim Brogan at left-back for the last half-hour.

On the Saturday prior to the return with Inter, a 3–0 victory at East Fife guaranteed Celtic a record seventh successive Scottish First Division title, one better than the great Celtic side who had won the League six consecutive times between 1905 and 1910. 'We have an uncomplicated method of play,' said Stein, 'which combines the discipline of a fluid 4–3–3 formation with allowing players to express themselves freely.

'We make changes frequently. That way, no one becomes complacent. Our young players know that they are going to be given their chance. So, in addition to a good scouting system, we have players coming to us because success breeds success and we are the club they want to be with. But for all our resources I wouldn't want to make any forecasts about next season's League title.' While praising his youngsters, Stein also paid tribute to older players such as Craig, Murdoch, Brogan, Lennox, Johnstone and McNeill.

'Big Jock was never the big, hard man I've seen him described as,' says Billy McNeill. 'He had a hard side to him and he could hurt you when he felt like it – he had a tongue that could cut you in bits. He could shout too. But there was a right soft side to him. He could get really bad tempered which, as far as I'm concerned, is an endearing factor. I hate people who have no passion and big Jock certainly had plenty of passion.

'I remember he once suspended Jimmy Johnstone. He sent him away from training for two weeks and said, "I don't want to see you near the place." Three days later, Jock says to me, "I want to talk to you. That wee man's been on the phone. I've not spoken to him but I'm thinking I'll maybe just phone him up and tell him it's all right to come back in."

'So he worried about that aspect of things. He could be sympathetic and, indeed, quite a soft man at times. He'd maybe punish people and think later on, "Maybe I shouldn't have done that." He could be a good counsel and a good father figure. He was a man of great contradictions, a very complex individual.'

Bobby Murdoch eases the ball away from two Hibernian challenges during the 1972 Scottish Cup Final.

Jim Craig also recalls Stein's strong nature. 'He could be very sharp with you but my wife had a couple of miscarriages and Jock sent cards and flowers and would constantly enquire as to how she was. Yet at the same time he might not be speaking to you for some reason or other. I suppose that's part and parcel of being a boss of any company. There's no point in being hard all the time – you've got to show you're human. That understanding of how to get the best out of people would all have been natural on Jock's part – that's what made it so good.'

Before their return with Celtic, Inter took up residence in Troon minus Roberto Boninsegna, who had injured an ankle at Fiorentina the previous Sunday. He had acted as the lone striker in the first leg of the European Cup semi-final and his absence left Sandro Mazzola, one of four Inter survivors from Lisbon, as the Italians' sole attacker. Stripped of their striker, Inter funnelled back into defence from the start of the second leg. For Celtic, Murdoch showed glimpses of genius but for youngsters such as Dalglish and Macari this appeared to be a game too far at this early stage in their careers.

Johnstone was so tightly marked by Oriali that the best he could do was pull his marker out of position on to the left wing. That left space for Craig to roam forward on the right. The full-back took full advantage of this, twice coming close to scoring in the early stages. McCluskey, who started in the left-back position, lacked the athleticism of Craig and Gemmell and was no overlapper. With McCluskey rarely causing attacking problems for Inter, Bobby Lennox, on the left wing, was unable to free himself from the skin-tight Italian marking.

Celtic failed to score an early goal and, with several of their players out of kilter, soon ran out of variety in their attacking moves. The Italians quickly adjusted their deeply defensive system of play to match. Celtic's best chance of the evening came when Inter centre-back Burgnich, another veteran of Lisbon, turned the ball against his own crossbar, but after extra-time it was still 0–0. The Celtic fans would now be treated to something completely different.

At a meeting of UEFA in Como, northern Italy, on the day of the 1970 European Cup Final, it had been agreed that penalty shoot-outs would be introduced to the competition from the 1970-1 season. These would be used to settle ties drawn on aggregate where the contestants could not be separated by away goals. As in 1967, Mazzola was the first man to hit the net, knocking his penalty past Evan Williams, who had been restored to the Celtic team in the second half of the season.

In training at Seamill, Dixie Deans had been the undisputed champion at penalty-kick practice. Against Inter, he had replaced Dalglish when he came on as a second-half substitute. The striker, on his first appearance in Europe, now ran up to take Celtic's first penalty, looking extremely confident. Hoping to hit the ball high over goalkeeper Vieri's left shoulder, Deans leaned back to get height on his kick … but he leaned back too far. His shot went over the bar and high into the dark Glasgow sky.

Frustalupi, Facchetti and Pellizzaro scored Inter's next three penalties. Craig, Johnstone and McCluskey did likewise for Celtic. Then Jair carefully guided his kick, Inter's fifth, to Williams' right and netted a place for the Italians in the European Cup Final. Stein had been in favour of the introduction of penalties when UEFA had made their rule change. Now, having seen the process in action, he described it as a 'circus act'.

'They were hardly up the park,' says Jimmy Johnstone. 'At one point I went away back to our own eighteen-yard line. I looked round and the guy marking me was standing behind me. They went everywhere with you! And if you got by them they would bodycheck you.'

Stein was soon looking to the future once again. 'We have too much going for ourselves to dwell on that game now. They beat us on a technicality but it will show our young players there is a lot more to European football. No one anticipated our team going as far in the competition this season although we are disappointed to go out at this stage.'

Two-and-a-half weeks later, on 6 May 1972, renewed resolve among the Celtic players was evident in the Scottish Cup Final with Hibernian. The 106,102 crowd had barely settled into their assorted positions around Hampden Park before Billy McNeill had glided in at Hibs' back post to sidefoot Celtic into the lead. Alan Gordon equalized for Hibs but from then on an exquisite display of attacking football provided Dixie Deans with a hat-trick and Lou Macari with a double. The 6–1 victory was the highest winning margin in a Scottish Cup Final in the twentieth century. It was also the first time any team had scored six in the Final since Renton had achieved that feat in 1888, the year in which Celtic was founded.

Jim Craig was to part company with Stein and Celtic in the summer of 1972. 'It's hard for somebody to realize the sheer charisma or the sheer presence of Jock,' says Craig, who completed his studies as a dentist shortly after turning professional with Celtic in the mid-1960s. 'He wasn't a particularly tall man – he was about 5ft10in – but he was very good at making his presence felt and you always knew who was boss. He had a certain presence. Certain people come into a room and you look at them automatically. He was an amazing man and it was an amazing time. We were very, very privileged to have been there at the time.'

At the end of the 1972 Scottish Cup Final, Stein showed his delight by speeding on to the pitch and hugging his players. With his zest for the game and a group of young players requiring his guidance Stein still had many reasons to look forward to the future as manager of Celtic Football Club.

# CHAPTER EIGHT
# TRIUMPHS AND TRIALS

MIDWAY THROUGH THE 1972-3 SEASON, JOCK STEIN EXPERIENCED THE RARE SENSATION OF EVENTS beginning to overtake him. In the opening days of January 1973, Lou Macari, still only twenty-three years old and barely established as a Celtic first-team regular, decided it was time to seek the financial security of a move to England. In December 1972 Tommy Docherty had resigned as Scotland manager to take over at Manchester United and had begun immediately signing Scots with whom he had worked at international level. Macari became his latest signing for a £200,000 fee, a record transfer for a Scottish player.

At Celtic Park, Macari had been earning around £60 per week. At Old Trafford he could take home approximately quadruple that figure. Stein had had to deal with discontented players in previous years but had always been able to pacify them when they were still of use to him. Once they were just past their prime, they would be sold off, bringing in a useful fee. The new generation of the 1970s was less willing to accept a wage structure falling further and further behind the pay available at the top clubs in England. The Celtic board, however, was unwilling to even contemplate changing its policy.

A lot of the new players certainly loved playing for Celtic and it must have been a great experience for them to come into a team of that quality in the early days of their careers. However, several would leave the club because they were pushing for pay and conditions that Stein, but more particularly the club, was not prepared to give them. In the 1960s most players had such a love of the club that they would sign a new contract with barely a glance, but Stein now had to negotiate wages with players who were much more financially aware. This was a draining experience and a potential source of bitter argument and disappointment between him and his players. Stein would then have to put on his motivator's hat to get the same players prepared for a match.

A fortnight before Christmas 1972 Macari had been part of the Celtic team that had lost a third successive League Cup Final. Hibs had exacted revenge for the previous spring's Scottish Cup Final defeat by beating Celtic 2–1 at Hampden Park. Celtic were also out of the European Cup by then, having been turned over by Ujpest Dozsa in the second round. After a 2–1 Celtic win at Parkhead, Stein had adopted a defensive formation in Budapest only to see Ujpest assemble a 3–0 lead by midway through the first half. The Celtic defence was shredded time and again even though no further goals were scored.

Most worryingly for Stein, three days after Christmas Day 1972 the Celtic manager was admitted to the Victoria Infirmary in Glasgow after complaining of feeling unwell. Officially he was suffering from a 'flu virus' but it was heart trouble that had necessitated Stein's twelve-day stay in hospital. In the Celtic dugout Stein would grimace through a game, wincing at every incident that brought his displeasure, occasionally bursting forth from his seat to let fly a mouthful of invective at an offending player.

Stein recuperated with a brief holiday in Aviemore. On 13 January, he was back at

Celtic goalkeeper Peter Latchford presents Billy McNeill – known as 'Caesar' by Celtic fans – with his laurels in the shape of a Celtic scarf. After ten years as Jock Stein's captain, the indomitable McNeill had announced his retirement. The 1975 Scottish Cup Final victory over Airdrie was his last appearance for the Celts and his team-mates acknowledged the moment by chairing him in celebration at the match's end. As Stein's trusted lieutenant on the field, McNeill had carried out his duties magnificently.

Celtic Park to watch from the directors' box as his team defeated Dundee 2–1. Celtic had been two points clear of Hibs and three clear of Rangers at Christmas, but in the wake of Stein's illness they had lost to Rangers at Ibrox at New Year and, in late January, reached the season's nadir with a 2–1 defeat at Airdrie that saw Celtic players arguing with one another as the game slipped away from them.

Having lost the leadership of the League to Rangers at the start of the year, Celtic were forced to adopt the role of chasers. In late March Kenny Dalglish, to whom Celtic looked more and more for inspiration, was injured but Celtic defeated Hearts and Falkirk to stay on Rangers' tail, two points behind with a game in hand. On Tuesday 3 April 1973, Motherwell came to Celtic Park for a League fixture. Fans, using the recently decimalized currency, paid 66 pence to enter the upper stand, which had been entirely refurbished in 1971. Handing over 44p obtained entry to a new front stand, which had replaced the standing enclosure. Payment of 33p brought entry to the terracing, which remained largely unchanged throughout the Stein years.

Against Motherwell, half-time came and went with no goals scored. Ten minutes after the break, Dalglish, hovering on the edge of the penalty area, took the ball on his chest, let it drop and swiped a left-footed shot into the Motherwell goal. With twenty minutes remaining, the same player cleverly clipped the ball across the face of goal for Deans to nudge it into the net. The 2–0 win took Celtic to the top of the League with a goal difference of plus fifty-one as opposed to Rangers' plus forty. Both Old Firm defences had conceded twenty-seven goals but Celtic's superior attack had accumulated off seventy-eight goals as opposed to Rangers' sixty-seven.

A replayed Scottish Cup semi-final with Dundee resulted in a 3–0 win for Celtic but allowed Rangers to re-establish a two-point lead in the League. Away to St Johnstone, on 16 April, Stein told his players to relax and enjoy their football. They did so, moving the ball about in patient, classy fashion, easing to a 3–1 win. 'It's in our hands now,' said the manager as he awaited Celtic's final three League games of the 1972-3 season. 'It's entirely up to the players. They know what is needed.'

Celtic players enjoy their lap of honour at Easter Road, Edinburgh, after clinching the club's eighth successive Scottish League title in April 1973. From left: Tommy Callaghan, Dixie Deans, Kenny Dalglish (partly obscured), Jimmy Johnstone, Danny McGrain, George Connelly (partly obscured), Bobby Murdoch, Billy McNeill, David Hay, Alistair Hunter.

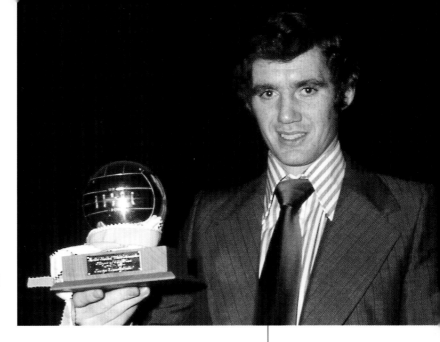

A 5–0 Celtic Park win over second-bottom Dumbarton bolstered Celtic's goal difference as Stein's men went top with two Saturdays to go. On the first, they smoothed their way to a 4–0 defeat of Arbroath while Rangers were drawing at Aberdeen. To take the title, Celtic needed only to draw at Hibernian on the final day of the League season. 'We most certainly won't play it safe and go for a draw against Hibs,' said Stein. 'That's not our style. We haven't achieved what we have by being defensively minded.'

Five days before the game, George Connelly was named Scotland's Player of the Year. The midfielder paid tribute to Stein for encouraging him to express himself on the pitch. In Edinburgh on 28 April an even greater tribute was paid to Stein as his players produced a performance in Celtic's traditional style to notch a 3–0 win. The exuberance of the Celtic players' celebrations on their lap of honour showed that winning an eighth successive title had produced no reduction in their enjoyment of an achievement that had now become a hardy annual.

Stein now felt that Celtic had emerged from their transitional period. He promised they would be even stronger for the 1973-4 season. 'I think those young players had a lot to thank the older ones for,' says Jimmy Johnstone of the lads who burst into the Celtic team in the late 1960s and early 1970s. 'It must have been great for them coming into an environment like that. We more or less took them by the hand. Coming into a bad team it's very difficult. Coming into a team that's on song like that makes it so easy. You had Victor Davidson, big Geordie Connelly, Davie Hay, Danny McGrain, Pat McCluskey, Jimmy Quinn, Kenny Dalglish. What a reserve side they made! They won the Reserve League two years in a row because they couldn't get a game in the first team!

'They came on by leaps and bounds. I'm not boasting but I think it was mainly due to us because we gave them so much encouragement. They could try something in a game and if it didn't happen we would say, "It's all right, son, it'll happen again. Don't worry about it." We'd give them the ball again. And that would give them a good feeling because they looked up to you. They'd go away home and tell their dad about it. I know, because I did it myself when I was just coming through and would maybe get a nod off of Willie Fernie or Bobby Collins.'

Stein's promise of progress was fulfilled. In the 1973-4 season Celtic once again reached the semi-finals of the European Cup, after victories over TPS Turku of Finland, Vejle Boldklub of Denmark and Basle of Switzerland. Their opponents in the semi-final were Atletico Madrid, the champions of Spain. Glasgow fans relished the glamour of a tie with representatives of one of Europe's most traditionally stylish footballing nations.

It proved the most unpleasant evening ever witnessed at Celtic Park. Atletico's Argentinian manager, Juan Carlos Lorenzo, had promised a physical encounter. His players, several of whom were also Argentinians, took him at his word. A vicious display

George Connelly shows off his Scottish Footballer of the Year award in 1973. At the age of twenty-four, Connelly appeared to have a potentially exceptional career ahead of him. Equally at ease in central defence or in midfield, Connelly was one of the most technically accomplished players ever to have graced the Celtic Park turf. However, his shyness meant the Fifer never truly settled in Glasgow. He also found it difficult to cope with the attention paid to a professional footballer at a big-city club. The 1972-73 campaign was to be his last full season in the Celtic team. After a string of absences and reappearances, the player would eventually leave Celtic Park and football in 1975 at the lamentably early age of twenty-six.

of fouling resulted in three Atletico players – Diaz, Quique and Ayala – being dismissed by Turkish referee Mr Babacan. Five others were cautioned. Of the Celtic players, only Deans and Brogan were booked. Those statistics told the tale of an evening when Celtic were impeded every time they appeared on the verge of getting a move together. It ended in a scoreless draw, the result Atletico had wanted. As the players left the pitch and headed for the tunnel, Atletico's Eusebio landed a punch on Jimmy Johnstone's head. Police intervened to keep the Atletico players from making further assaults on Stein's men.

Stein commented afterwards: 'The people I feel sorry for are the fans who paid big money to see what should have been a classic game. They ended up not seeing a game at all. Atletico simply didn't want to play and they went out to make sure we didn't play either. I was happy with the way our players and supporters refused to become involved in any of the trouble. They showed great restraint when they had been badly provoked.'

'Big Jock met the manager of the Argentinian national team at the World Cup that summer,' says Jimmy Johnstone. 'He said that if they had been dope tested, five or six of that Atletico team would have been found to have been using stimulants. They were just mad, nutters.'

Celtic waited for UEFA to decide the punishment for Atletico Madrid. Instead, European football's governing body limply warned Atletico that similar scenes in Madrid to those in Glasgow would result in 'ultimate sanctions'. It had, of course, never been likely that the Spanish club would approach their home leg in the same fashion as they had gone about their task at Celtic Park.

Desmond White issued a statement on behalf of Celtic on 18 April, six days before the scheduled return leg in Madrid. 'The Celtic board have studied closely the decision of UEFA. We are completely mystified by its terms and consider it to be both illogical and unjust. After giving careful consideration to the views of our own supporters and the football public in general, and our obligations to the game of football, we have decided to fulfil the fixture under protest and have advised UEFA accordingly.'

A police escort met the Celtic party at Madrid Airport and remained with them throughout their stay. It was necessary to protect the players from the Atletico fans, who had been riled by outraged Spanish newspaper accounts of the proceedings at the first leg in Glasgow. An armed guard patrolled the grounds of the Hotel Monte Royal, where Celtic were staying. On trips to training, the Celtic coach would be followed by jeering, spitting fans. 'Hatred surrounded us from the moment we arrived in Madrid to the moment we left,' says Jimmy Johnstone.

'I don't think we should have been asked to play the game here,' Stein had said on Celtic's arrival in the Spanish capital. 'UEFA only kicked around the problem.' For the second leg, Atletico banned the sale of alcohol inside their stadium. Cushions were also withdrawn from sale: these were traditionally sold to Spanish fans to aid their comfort but would be thrown on to the pitch when the fans were displeased with their team's performance. It was the first time in Atletico's history that such steps had been taken. Prior to the match, both Jock Stein and Jimmy Johnstone received phone calls at their hotel issuing them with death threats. Stein, ignoring the clamour surrounding the game, said: 'We feel we can win if we are allowed to play football.'

Six of Atletico's hard men had been suspended after doing their job at Celtic Park. Lorenzo, as he had almost certainly planned all along, brought in some of his more skilful players for the return in the Vicente Calderon Stadium. 'We have never wanted to win a game more,' said Stein, exasperated with both UEFA's hands-off approach to the tie and with the enervating conditions with which Celtic had to cope in Madrid. 'It's not so much that we want to reach another European Cup Final but because we dearly want to deprive Atletico of any chance of winning it – a Cup they have dishonoured, a tournament of which they have made a farce.'

On the night, mounted police were employed to keep Atletico fans their distance from the Celtic players as they left their coach for the dressing room. The pitch was ringed by riot police. Atletico were terrified of the consequences of further violence in the tie. Celtic, as always, were looking to play a fair game within the rules. With the Spanish team's good side showing, the second leg soon became an absorbing, then a thrilling football match.

The first clear chance fell to Kenny Dalglish. Showing swift reflexes, he twisted on to a clever pass from overlapping right-back Danny McGrain. The forward's shot sped goalwards but was diverted round the post by Atletico goalkeeper Reina. Atletico's response was swift, an equally precise shot from centre-back Capon spearing towards the roof of the Celtic net until Denis Connaghan rose to hold it with some aplomb.

The football continued to flow but half-time arrived with the score still 0–0. Lennox and Johnstone went close after the break, but then a sequence of scoring chances fell Atletico's way. Celtic held firm but the pressure intensified. Atletico, roared on by 65,000 demented supporters, continued to act as picadors to Celtic's bullish defence, prodding and probing for weaknesses.

The Celtic-Atletico Madrid European Cup semi-final first leg in April 1974 totters on the edge of anarchy after another in a succession of fouls on Jimmy Johnstone, who lies injured. Billy McNeill rounds angrily on Atletico players while Harry Hood pleads for justice with Turkish referee Dogan Babacan.

David Hay challenges Atletico Madrid's Garate during the second leg of the semi-final with Atletico. Garate would be the architect of the Spanish team's victory on a night when they resorted to football after having killed the first leg stone dead.

Eventually, Celtic's resistance was worn down. With fifteen minutes to go, Garate worked some space for himself in front of goal and pushed the ball into the Celtic net. Atletico now went for the kill. With four minutes to go, Garate put the ball into Abelardo's path. The midfielder sent the ball high into the Celtic net and the Glasgow club were out of the 1974 European Cup.

Three days after the match in Madrid, Celtic took hold of their ninth successive Scottish League title. A cleverly curled Kenny Dalglish shot gave them their goal in a 1–1 draw at Falkirk and they ended the season four points clear of second-placed Hibernian. It saw Celtic equal the world record for successive title wins that had, until then, been held jointly by MTK Budapest of Hungary and CSKA Sofia of Bulgaria. However, Celtic were unique in having blended domestic success with consistent excellence in European competition.

That 1973-4 season also saw Celtic appear in their sixth successive Scottish Cup Final. One year previously, Celtic had unluckily lost 3–2 to Rangers in the Final and then, later in 1973, they had lost 1–0 to Dundee in the League Cup Final. On 4 May 1974, confronted by Dundee United in the Scottish Cup Final, Celtic eased to a 3–0 win. Later that year, Celtic would make their tenth consecutive appearance in the League Cup Final, defeating Hibs 6–3. Of the twenty domestic Cup Finals that had taken place since Stein's arrival as Celtic manager, Celtic had appeared in nineteen of them, winning twelve.

The afternoon of that League Cup victory over Hibs at Hampden produced scenes of delirious joy among the Celtic fans in the 54,000 crowd. An exuberant hat-trick from the burly Dixie Deans had seen Celtic overwhelm Hibs with some excellent attacking football. It helped to temporarily erase the memory of Celtic's premature exit from their ninth European Cup competition just three weeks previously.

After an uninspiring 1–1 draw with Greek champions Olympiakos in Glasgow, Celtic were beaten 2–0 in Athens. Although the playing surface had been poor Olympiakos were European opponents of only average ability. In the second leg, the central defensive partnership of Billy McNeill and Pat McCluskey had looked shaky. McNeill, now thirty-four years old, was making errors that would have been unimaginable in his prime.

George Connelly, a country boy from Fife who never managed to adjust to the pressures of big-city football, was experiencing ongoing off-field difficulties. David Hay, after an excellent World Cup for Scotland in the summer of 1974, had joined Macari in hitting the trail south, joining Chelsea for £250,000. Jimmy Johnstone, Kenny Dalglish and Danny McGrain, all of whom had been with Scotland at the 1974 World Cup in West Germany, had begun the 1974-5 season looking jaded.

Celtic still managed to lead the Scottish First Division by two points as they entered 1975 but at Ibrox, on 4 January, they were beaten 3–0. They retained their League lead but only briefly – a series of disastrous results followed in the second half of the season. After the Rangers match Celtic won just four more League games, drawing three and losing seven. Stein's side ended up in third place, eleven points behind champions Rangers and four below second-placed Hibs.

They still had enough ability to win the Scottish Cup, beating Airdrie 3–1 in the 1975 Final but this was meagre compensation for Celtic fans, who were used to partaking of rich fare at the top table in Europe. After the Airdrie match, Billy McNeill retired as a player. 'Big Jock and I always had a good relationship,' says the man who was Stein's captain for a decade. 'He put additional demands on me. I had to act in such a way that I sorted things out when he wasn't about; when he went out of the dressing room, when we went on the pitch.

'When we went away and started enjoying ourselves I had to be an influencing factor, which didn't bother me. We had a real hard, aggressive squad of players, some with real strong personalities but it wasn't important for me to be liked by everybody. What was important was that they respected my position, which they did do. And it was important that I respected their point of view as well. I was the captain but in effect we had another four or five people who could have performed as captain as well.

'The bulk of the players would have wanted nothing other than to play for Celtic. We had a magnificent team spirit. We enjoyed each others' company. I'm not saying we were the greatest pals – we weren't. But we had a feeling and a pride in our achievements and we enjoyed the fact that we could take on the best on the European scene and do well.'

That summer Jimmy Johnstone, at the age of thirty, also left Celtic, on a free transfer. To the Celtic support it 'felt like the end of an era. It was the end of an era. 'The team that won the European Cup were superb, a one-off,' says Jimmy Johnstone. 'In later years it

Kenny Dalglish scores one of his 166 goals in a Celtic jersey, with Hibs his victims on this occasion. It is a measure of the player's superior concentration that he is able to remember in detail his many goals. The forward's shimmies, flicks and spatial awareness made him unique. Entirely elusive, he was a player of a type not previously seen in Scotland. Rather than strength or speed, Dalglish relied on his quick football brain and timing for his marvellous creativity. His roving eye for a pass or a shot made him close to impossible for opponents to cope with.

Jimmy Johnstone opens the scoring for Celtic against Hibs in the 1974 Scottish League Cup Final. The winger's goal would be followed by a Dixie Deans hat-trick in the 6-3 win. It was the second time in two years Celtic had hit six in a final against Hibs. On both occasions Deans had scored a hat-trick.

was like somebody trying to copy someone singing or something like that. You try but you can't beat the original. That team was something else. I don't think they'll ever have a team as good as 1967 – especially as they were all home-grown. All round I have never seen a team that had as much talent throughout the side. Ajax, with Cruyff, Neeskens and all them were tremendous but they would maybe have five stars who ran the team. All eleven of us played our parts.'

The summer of 1975 compounded Celtic's problems. Jock Stein met with near-tragedy. Returning from a summer holiday in Minorca, Stein, his wife Jean and friends were motoring north after having flown in to Manchester. Stein was at the wheel of a Mercedes. In the early morning of Saturday 5 July the Mercedes collided head-on with another car on the A74 at Lockerbie. Stein was rushed to intensive care at Dumfries infirmary. During a life-saving operation, an incision was made in his windpipe to help him breathe.

The head and chest injuries he had sustained in the crash meant that Stein remained in intensive care for a month. He required serious recuperation and did not return to Celtic Park as manager until the summer of 1976. In his absence, Sean Fallon served as acting manager during the 1975-6 season. For the first time since 1963-4, Celtic failed to win a trophy.

There was further bad news for Celtic in early August 1975, when Kenny Dalglish requested a transfer. Dalglish had a genuine affection for the club and its supporters but was dissatisfied with the terms he had been offered. The most talented of the players who had replaced the Lisbon Lions, it was a mark of his loyalty to the Celtic fans and to Jock Stein that he had remained at Celtic Park long after contemporaries of lesser ability had left. By the mid-1970s, however, he had lost patience with Celtic's archaic wage structure although eventually there was a reconciliation between the player and the club.

On his return to Celtic Park for the 1976-7 season, Jock Stein appeared to be a changed man. Prior to the League Cup Final with Aberdeen in November 1976 he spoke of how he wished only that the game was a good one and that the supporters of both sides would enjoy the spectacle put before them. This seemed to be a less gritty Stein than the determined winner who had done everything in his power to make Celtic close to unbeatable in his first decade at the club. His side dominated the match but lost 2–1 to Aberdeen in an entertaining final.

'The car crash seemed to take his enthusiasm away,' says Billy McNeill, 'and it seemed to take his personality away to a degree. He never quite seemed the same big, enthusiastic, outgoing personality that he had been. It probably encouraged him to think of himself and to look after himself more than anything else.'

Stein still had the ability to produce a masterstroke. In September 1976, he had signed

Pat Stanton from Hibernian, with centre-back Jackie McNamara moving to Edinburgh in exchange. Stanton, a central defender-cum-sweeper, was approaching his thirty-second birthday but his game had always been based on brain rather than brawn. He relied on his clever reading of play to get to the ball before faster players. His passing was fascinatingly accurate; over a match it was unusual to see even one Stanton pass fail to find its intended target.

The experience of Stanton steadied a young, fresh Celtic team. Of the Lisbon Lions, only Bobby Lennox, now thirty-three, remained and he started only two League matches that season. To Stanton's right, the centre-back could rely entirely on Danny McGrain, a twenty-six year old who was rapidly establishing himself as the finest full-back in the world. McGrain combined consistency with courage and imagination. His overlapping runs spurred Celtic into devastating attacks while his defensive game was immaculate. Solid tackling and perfect positioning made it close to impossible for opponents to bypass him.

Further forward, Roy Aitken, a powerfully built seventeen year old, performed manfully as the holding player in midfield. Ronnie Glavin, a twenty-five year old who had been signed from Partick Thistle for £80,000 in 1974, provided drive in that area of the park. Dalglish, still only twenty-five, continued to improve year on year. For the attack, Stein signed twenty-two year old Joe Craig from Partick Thistle for £60,000 in September 1976. A pleasingly direct striker, Craig fitted seamlessly into the side, responding well to the promptings of Dalglish and Glavin. Wide on the right, Stein had a traditional type of winger in Johnny Doyle, a twenty-five year old who had been Celtic's record signing when purchased from Ayr United for £90,000 in March 1976.

Teenager Tommy Burns made a notable contribution in midfield as did Paul Wilson, a twenty-five year old Scots-Indian who had scored two of Celtic's goals in the 1975 Scottish Cup Final. Stein also made one of his most intriguing signings that season when he brought twenty-four year old Alfie Conn back to Scotland from Tottenham Hotspur. Conn had signed for Spurs three years previously from rivals Rangers.

Stanton and Craig had been cup-tied for the League Cup Final but when they were restored to the side Stein began to push his men towards the title. Three months later, in February 1977, Celtic scored eleven goals in seven days, defeating Hibs, Hearts and Partick Thistle in the process. It took Celtic four points clear of Aberdeen with a game in hand. 'Most of these boys would be winning the League for the first time,' said Stein. 'They are hungry for success, hungry for more victories.'

Scotland's top teams were by now playing for a new title, League football having been reconstructed in 1975. The First Division of eighteen clubs had been replaced by a Premier Division of ten clubs who were to play each other four times a season instead of the traditional twice. Reconstruction had been prompted largely by Celtic's domination of the League between the mid-1960s and the mid-1970s. With Stein at the helm again, the League title, regardless of the new format, again appeared destined for Celtic Park.

By late March, Rangers and Aberdeen were almost out of contention for the title. Dundee United were now Celtic's closest challengers. The Tannadice side were three points behind Celtic although Stein's side had a game in hand when Dundee United

Tea and Coca-Cola in the Easter Road dressing room in April 1977 after a 1-0 win over Hibs had ensured Jock Stein his tenth Scottish League title as Celtic manager. Back row, from left: Danny McGrain, Pat Stanton, Andy Lynch, Roy Aitken, Ronnie Glavin.
Front row: Joe Craig, Alfie Conn, Johnny Doyle, Tommy Burns, Roddie MacDonald.

visited Celtic Park on 26 March 1977 with 37,000 watching. United, unbeaten in ten games, were impressive from the start, spinning the ball around neatly from foot to foot.

In the twenty-fifth minute United's steady stream of passes brought them an advantage. McGrain tripped United forward Paul Hegarty inside the penalty area and United's penalty-taking goalkeeper Hamish McAlpine came forward to take the kick. As he prepared to run at the ball, the Celtic goalkeeper, Englishman Roy Baines, stepped forward from his line, making as if to clear a divot from the edge of the six-yard box. This piece of gamesmanship appeared to distract McAlpine and his weak penalty was saved.

On half-time, Conn's high cross from the right wing was greeted by Craig in front of goal with a solid header to make it 1–0 to Celtic. The Celts grew stronger and midway through the second half Doyle was manhandled off the ball by McAlpine. Glavin put the penalty kick behind the goalkeeper for a 2–0 win. Stein, twelve years into the job of Celtic manager, maintained his 'one game at a time' philosophy. 'That's another two points and another huge stride towards the title,' he said. 'But the championship is not over yet.'

Three weeks later, Celtic tied up the title when a Joe Craig goal gave them a 1–0 win over Hibs at Easter Road. Afterwards Stein and captain Kenny Dalglish celebrated by drinking Coca-Cola. 'It's a whole new ball game for these boys,' said Stein, 'and they can only improve. Only two of this side – Danny McGrain and Kenny Dalglish – had previously won championship medals.

'It is difficult to compare this present side with the one which won the European Cup in Lisbon ten years ago. Mind you, that team won the trophy at the first time of asking. They, too, were inexperienced at that level. I have had to patch this side at different stages this season, with players like Stanton, Craig and Conn. Next term they will have had the benefit of a summer tour and pre-season training behind them. We go to Australia and Singapore in July and we should be even better prepared for next season.'

The season ended satisfyingly with a 1–0 win over Rangers in the 1977 Scottish Cup Final. In the six months since losing to Aberdeen in the League Cup Final Celtic had lost just two matches, one at Aberdeen and one at Motherwell. It was an impressive record in a top division that no longer featured the weaker Scottish clubs.

Sadly, Stein's plans for the 1977-8 season were to be destroyed by the worst run of luck to befall him during his managership of Celtic. Before the season began, Kenny Dalglish again asked for a transfer. The player had asked away in the summer of 1976 but again had been persuaded to stay. As Celtic prepared for their close-season tour to Australia, Dalglish told Stein he would not be in the touring party. He had decided he wanted to test himself by playing in the English League. Over the summer Dalglish trained with the reserves and when Celtic returned from tour the player reiterated to Stein that he wished to leave.

The position with Dalglish remained the same as Celtic began their pre-season itinerary. Stein, however, remained hopeful of persuading his club captain to stay at Celtic Park. On 9 August Celtic travelled to Dunfermline for a friendly. Danny McGrain was made captain. As the team took the field, Jock Stein looked on with visible sadness. He knew that this would be the last time he would see Kenny Dalglish grace a football field in the hoops of Celtic. Later that evening Dalglish signed for Liverpool for a British record transfer fee of £440,000. Dalglish desired success in Europe and his decision to depart hinted that the player believed that the 1977 champions of Scotland were not capable of matching their predecessors in European competition.

'I think one of the things that annoyed big Jock, and possibly took something from him,' says Billy McNeill, 'was that the Dalglishs and the Macaris and the Hays fought him to get away. Until then he always had players who had wanted to play for him and stay with him. They would leave the club only when he wanted to transfer them. All of a sudden he had players who wanted away from Celtic Park regardless of his attempts to persuade them to stay. He saw them slide away from his influence.'

The following Saturday, 13 August 1977, Dalglish turned out for Liverpool in the Charity Shield at Wembley. Interviewed immediately after the game, he paid tribute to the club he had just left. The same afternoon, at Celtic Park, Pat Stanton was forced to leave the field through a knee injury in Celtic's opening game of the season, a 0–0 draw with Dundee United. It would prove to be his final game of the season and of his Celtic career. Severely weakened by the loss of two key players, Celtic suffered four defeats in their opening five League games.

On 1 October, Danny McGrain collided with Hibernian's John Blackley in a League match at Celtic Park. A resultant crippling foot injury saw the new Celtic captain miss the remainder of the season, a further crushing blow to Stein. McGrain had also suffered a fractured skull in 1972 and, in 1974, following the World Cup, had been diagnosed as a diabetic. McGrain had bravely come back from those misfortunes and he would beat the ankle problem but for the moment his absence left Celtic lacking experience and leadership on the field.

McGrain had been part of the Celtic side that had successfully negotiated their 1977-8 European Cup first-round tie with Jeunesse d'Esch of Luxembourg, winning 11–1 on aggregate but he was missing on 19 October 1977 as Celtic lined up against SW Innsbruck, the Austrian champions, at Celtic Park. Celtic's great European tradition, established during the Stein years, means that on European nights an infectious, incurable optimism affects every true Celtic supporter. The 30,000 present saw Celtic suffer some shaky moments and the tie was level at 1–1 with thirteen minutes remaining. Then the red-headed youngster Tommy Burns balanced himself beautifully to send a shot searing into the Austrians' net. It was a goal in which any Lisbon Lion would have taken pride. Overall, however, Celtic's performance was far from convincing.

Despite the massive sum of money taken in from the transfer of Kenny Dalglish and the subsequent injuries to key men Stanton and McGrain Stein was not given lavish funds to spend on new players. September 1977 had seen just the signings of Tom McAdam, a forward, at a cost of £60,000 from Dundee United and John Dowie, a midfielder, for £25,000 from Fulham. McAdam proved a willing worker. Johnny Doyle, at £90,000, remained Stein's record signing.

Frank Munro, a thirty year old central defender, was brought from Wolves, initially on loan for two months before being signed for £20,000. Full-back Joe Fillipi arrived from Ayr United for a tiny fee. Munro, who looked as though he was carrying excess weight, was less than a success and left the club at the end of the 1977-8 season. Fillipi and Dowie failed to establish themselves as regulars in the Celtic side. Stein's signing of Stanton had been a clever one but an exception to the rule that in the football transfer market you get what you pay for. The Celtic board's policy of selling high and buying cheap was beginning to look ridiculous.

Despite the fateful demolition of his team, Stein remained upbeat as he approached the second leg with Innsbruck. 'It is really a case of us not having the experience to play it tight but our boys have no reason to fear Innsbruck. We are a goal ahead and it is up to them to open out a bit to try to get on level terms. If they do that, they must leave gaps at the back and if our strikers are on form then the goals will come.'

After half an hour Celtic were 3–0 down, the defence having been punished severely for a series of basic errors. That remained the score at the end of a match that was disfigured by the usual Austrian gamesmanship. It was Celtic's least distinguished performance in Europe and three months later, in February 1978, Celtic plummeted to eighth position in the ten-team Premier Division. Now severely in danger of sinking into one of the two relegation spots, they were ahead of ninth-placed Ayr United only on goal difference.

A slight improvement in form saw Celtic go into the final day of the season, 29 April 1978, needing a win at St Mirren to guarantee a UEFA Cup place for 1978-9. A desolate performance led to a 3–1 defeat and a final placing of fifth in the Premier Division. It was Celtic's lowest placing since the 1964-5 season and the first time they had missed out on European competition since 1961-2. Jock Stein's team selection that day was: Latchford, Sneddon, Lynch, Edvaldsson, MacDonald, Aitken, Glavin, Mackie, McAdam, Conroy, McCluskey. It was a raw, inexperienced team with an average age of just twenty-two.

The following month, Jock Stein asked Billy McNeill if he would consider taking over from him as Celtic manager. The two men left the function they were attending in the MacDonald Hotel, Giffnock, to discuss the matter further. McNeill followed Stein's car then hopped in at Davieland Road to mull over the matter. There, in the shadow of the

bandstand in Rouken Glen park, Jock Stein made a verbal agreement with his former captain that he would take over from Jock Stein as Celtic manager.

'He said, "I want you to come back and be manager of Celtic," ' remembers Billy McNeill. 'It came as a total surprise to me. He had had a very poor season and I just took it that he had had enough at that level. He told me he was stepping away from it. I think it was his decision. Otherwise he would never have come to me and spoken to me about whether I wanted the job. He was the only one I spoke to about it and he seemed to be in charge of the whole situation. I thought that was going to be his mandate – to be in a more directorial role. Within weeks big Jock was away as well. Something suitable for him, something important and powerful, should have been put in place. The manner in which he left Celtic must have hurt him a lot.'

Stein had been given the offer of a directorial role at Celtic with special responsibility for Celtic Pools. Instead of taking it up, he accepted an offer from Leeds United to be manager at Elland Road. Stein, as so often, kept his own counsel on whether he felt the board's offer to him was a suitable one for a man of his stature.

On 29 May 1978 Billy McNeill resigned as manager of Aberdeen in order to take over from Jock Stein at Celtic. As his assistant he would bring with him his right-hand man from the Lisbon Lions – John Clark. Jock Stein's dynasty would live on at Celtic Park.

A testimonial for Stein, against Liverpool in August 1978, saw Celtic Park throbbing with a crowd unseen since the days when Celtic had been a powerful force in European football. Before the kick-off Stein was reunited with his Lisbon Lions and with Kenny Dalglish. Happiness beamed from Stein's features. The testimonial over, Stein swiftly left for his new job in England. The man who had embodied Celtic during the most successful era in the club's history had departed physically from Celtic Park but his spirit would remain an integral part of the club in the decades to come.

Joe Craig stays on his toes in the hope of a mistake from Rangers goalkeeper Stewart Kennedy in the 1977 Scottish Cup Final at Hampden. A penalty kick from Celtic left-back Andy Lynch proved the only goal of a drab Final. On a day of incessant drizzle, the crowd was reduced to just under 55,000 by the novelty of live televized transmission, the first time a Scottish Cup Final had been shown 'live' since the 1950s.

AN ALPHABET OF THE CELTS
by Eugene MacBride, Martin O'Connor and George Sheridan,
ACL Colour Print & Polar Publishing, Leicester, 1994

CELTIC 1888-1998: THE OFFICIAL ILLUSTRATED HISTORY
Graham McColl,
Hamlyn, London, 1998

THE CELTIC FOOTBALL COMPANION
David Docherty
John Donald Publishers Ltd, Edinburgh, 1986

Another trophy won, another day's work done. Jock Stein waves to fans from the Celtic team coach as it leaves Hampden Park following the 3-1 Scottish Cup Final win over Airdrie in 1975.